Radical Changes by Education

Radical Changes by Education

Edited by
Dr.S.K.PANNEER SELVAM
Assistant Professor, Department of Education
Bharathidasan University, Tiruchirappalli, Tamil Nadu

RANDOM PUBLICATIONS
NEW DELHI (INDIA)

Radical Changes by Education

ISBN 978-93-5111-351-5

Published in 2014 in India by

RANDOM PUBLICATIONS

4376-A/4B, Gali Murari Lal, Ansari Road
New Delhi-110 002
Phone: +9111-43580356, 23289044
E-mail: randomexports@gmail.com; sales@randompublications.com; info@randompublications.com

Type Setting by : Shah Computer Graphics, Delhi-110094
Digitally Printed at : Replika Press Pvt. Ltd.

Contents

1
Radical Changes by Education

1. Radical Changes by Education

1

Introduction

HISTORY OF INDIA, AN OVERVIEW

The people of India have had a continuous civilization since 2500 B.C., when the inhabitants of the Indus River valley developed an urban culture based on commerce and sustained by agricultural trade. This civilization declined around 1500 B.C., probably due to ecological changes. During the second millennium B.C., pastoral, Aryan-speaking tribes migrated from the northwest into the subcontinent. As they settled in the middle Ganges River valley, they adapted to antecedent cultures. The political map of ancient and medieval India was made up of myriad kingdoms with fluctuating boundaries. In the 4th and 5th centuries A.D., northern India was unified under the Gupta Dynasty. During this period, known as India's Golden Age, Hindu culture and political administration reached new heights.

Islam spread across the Indian subcontinent over a period of 500 years. In the 10th and 11th centuries, Turks and Afghans invaded India and established sultanates in Delhi. In the early 16th century, descendants of Genghis Khan swept across the

Khyber Pass and established the Mughal (Mogul) Dynasty, which lasted for 200 years. From the 11th to the 15th centuries, southern India was dominated by Hindu Chola and Vijayanagar Dynasties. During this time, the two systems—the prevailing Hindu and Muslim—mingled, leaving lasting cultural influences on each other.

The first British outpost in South Asia was established in 1619 at Surat on the northwestern coast. Later in the century, the East India Company opened permanent trading stations at Madras, Bombay, and Calcutta, each under the protection of native rulers. The British expanded their influence from these footholds until, by the 1850s, they controlled most of present-day India, Pakistan, and Bangladesh. In 1857, a rebellion in north India led by mutinous Indian soldiers caused the British Parliament to transfer all political power from the East India Company to the Crown. Great Britain began administering most of India directly while controlling the rest through treaties with local rulers.

In the late 1800s, the first steps were taken toward self-government in British India with the appointment of Indian councilors to advise the British viceroy and the establishment of provincial councils with Indian members; the British subsequently widened participation in legislative councils. Beginning in 1920, Indian leader Mohandas K. Gandhi transformed the Indian National Congress political party into a mass movement to campaign against British colonial rule. The party used both parliamentary and nonviolent resistance and non-cooperation to achieve independence. On August 15, 1947, India became a dominion within the Commonwealth, with Jawaharlal Nehru as Prime Minister. Enmity between Hindus and Muslims led the British to partition British India, creating East and West Pakistan, where there were Muslim majorities. India became a republic within the Commonwealth after promulgating its constitution on January 26, 1950.

After independence, the Congress Party, the party of Mahatma Gandhi and Jawaharlal Nehru, ruled India under the influence first of Nehru and then his daughter and grandson, with the exception of two brief periods in the 1970s and 1980s. Prime Minister Nehru governed India until his death in 1964. He was succeeded by Lal Bahadur Shastri, who also died in office. In 1966, power passed to Nehru's daughter, Indira Gandhi, Prime Minister from 1966 to 1977. In 1975, beset with deepening political and economic problems, Mrs. Gandhi declared a state of emergency and suspended many civil liberties. Seeking a mandate at the polls for her policies, she called for elections in 1977, only to be defeated by Moraji Desai, who headed the Janata Party, an amalgam of five opposition parties. In 1979, Desai's Government crumbled. Charan Singh formed an interim government, which was followed by Mrs. Gandhi's return to power in January 1980. On October 31, 1984, Mrs. Gandhi was assassinated, and her son, Rajiv, was chosen by the Congress (I)—for "Indira"—Party to take her place. His government was brought down in 1989 by allegations of corruption and was followed by V.P. Singh and then Chandra Shekhar.

In the 1989 elections, although Rajiv Gandhi and Congress won more seats in the 1989 elections than any other single party; he was unable to form a government with a clear majority. The Janata Dal, a union of opposition parties, was able to form a government with the help of the Hindu-nationalist Bharatiya Janata Party (BJP) on the right and the communists on the left. This loose coalition collapsed in November 1990, and the government was controlled for a short period by a breakaway Janata Dal group supported by Congress (I), with Chandra Shekhar as Prime Minister. That alliance also collapsed, resulting in national elections in June 1991. On May 27, 1991, while campaigning in Tamil Nadu on behalf of Congress (I), Rajiv Gandhi was assassinated, apparently by Tamil extremists from Sri Lanka. In the elections, Congress (I) won 213 parliamentary seats and put together a coalition, returning to power under the leadership of P.V. Narasimha Rao. This Congress-led government, which served a full 5-year term, initiated a gradual process of economic liberalization and reform, which has opened the Indian economy to global trade and investment. India's domestic politics also took new shape, as traditional alignments by caste, creed, and ethnicity gave way to a plethora of small, regionally based political parties.

The final months of the Rao-led government in the spring of 1996 were marred by several major political corruption scandals, which contributed to the worst electoral performance by the Congress Party in its history. The Hindu-nationalist Bharatiya Janata Party (BJP) emerged from the May 1996 national elections as the single-largest party in the Lok Sabha but without enough strength to prove a majority on the floor of that Parliament. Under Prime Minister Atal Bihari Vajpayee, the BJP coalition lasted in power 13 days. With all political parties wishing to avoid another round of elections, a 14-party coalition led by the Janata Dal emerged to form a government known as the United Front, under the former Chief Minister of Karnataka, H.D. Deve Gowda. His government lasted less than a year, as the leader of the Congress Party withdrew his support in March 1997. Inder Kumar Gujral replaced Deve Gowda as the consensus choice for Prime Minister of a 16-party United Front coalition. In November 1997, the Congress Party in India again withdrew support for the United Front. New elections in February 1998 brought the BJP the largest number of seats in Parliament—182—but fell far short of a majority. On March 20, 1998, the President inaugurated a BJP-led coalition government with Vajpayee again serving as Prime Minister. On May 11 and 13, 1998, this government conducted a series of underground nuclear tests forcing U.S. President Clinton to impose economic sanctions on India pursuant to the 1994 Nuclear Proliferation Prevention Act.

In April 1999, the BJP-led coalition government fell apart, leading to fresh elections in September. The National Democratic Alliance-a new coalition led by the BJP-gained a majority to form the government with Vajpayee as Prime Minister in October 1999. Now Sri Manmohan Singh is a Prime Minister of India. The Government was formed in 2004. This is called as UPA (United Progressive Alliance). The Chairperson of UPA is Mss. Sonia Gandhi.

CORRUPTION - INTRODUCTION

Corruption is a universal phenomenon. It is not something new either. Corruption in one form or another existed since time immemorial. A review of penal codes utilized in various ancient civilizations clearly demonstrate that bribery was a serious problem among the Jews, the Chinese, the Japanese, the Greeks, the Romans as well as the Aztees of the New World (Thakur, 1979:7). In ancient India large-scale corruption dominated public life (Thakur, 1979:12). As has been observed "corruption prevailed on a larger scale in India during the ancient period and the ones that followed" (Padhay 1986:26). From this one can assume the nature and scale in the increase of corruption from medieval to the present time in the countries of the Indian sub-continent. One of the greatest evils of medieval administration in India was the extortion of perquisites and presents (Sarkar, 1935:83). Corruption was evident during the British rule in India. There was almost regular and systematic corruption involving almost all officials at different levels in the political and administrative hierarchy. There was an underlying belief among officials of "making hay while the sun of British Raj shone" (Dwivedi and Bhargava, 1967:7).

CORRUPTION - SYNONYMS, RELATED WORDS AND ANTONYMS

A) Noun

1. Corruption - lack of integrity or honesty (especially susceptibility to bribery); use of a position of trust for dishonest gain corruptness.

   Infection - moral corruption or contamination; "ambitious men are led astray by an infection that is almost unavoidable".

   Venality - prostitution of talents or offices or services for reward.

   Dishonesty - the quality of being dishonest.

   Jobbery - corruptness among public officials.

2. Corruption - in a state of progressive putrefaction, Putrescence, putrid ness, rottenness, Putrefaction, rot - decay usually accompanied by an offensive odor
3. Corruption - decay of matter (as by rot or oxidation)

   Decay - the process of gradually becoming inferior
4. corruption - moral perversion; impairment of virtue and moral principles; "the luxury and corruption among the upper classes"; "moral degeneracy followed intellectual degeneration"; "its brothels; its opium parlors; its depravity". Depravity, degeneracy Immorality - the quality of not being in accord with standards of right or good conduct; "the immorality of basing the defense of the West on the threat of mutual assured destruction".
5. Corruption - destroying someone's (or some group's) honesty or loyalty; undermining moral integrity; "corruption of a minor"; "the big city's subversion of rural innocence". Subversion, Degradation, debasement - changing to a lower state (a less respected state).
6. Corruption - inducement (as of a public official) by improper means (as bribery) to violate duty (as by committing a felony); "he was held on charges of corruption and racketeering".

   Inducing, inducement - act of bringing about a desired result; "inducement of sleep".
7. Degrading, immoral acts or habits: bestiality, depravity, flagitiousness, immorality, perversion, turpitude, vice, villainous ness, villainy, wickedness. See clean/dirty.
8. Departure from what is legally, ethically, and morally correct: corruptness, dishonesty, improbity. Informal crookedness. See honest/dishonest.
9. A term that offends against established usage standards: barbarism, solecism, vulgarism. See style/good style/bad style.

(B) CORRUPTION - MEANINGS

Meaning 1: lack of integrity or honesty (especially susceptibility to bribery); use of a position of trust for dishonest gain

Synonym: corruptness

Meaning 2: in a state of progressive putrefaction

Synonyms: putrescence, putrid ness, rottenness

Meaning 3: decay of matter (as by rot or oxidation)

Meaning 4: moral perversion; impairment of virtue and moral principles; its opium parlors; its depravity"

Synonyms: degeneracy, depravity

Meaning 5: destroying someone's (or some group's) honesty or loyalty; undermining moral integrity

Synonym: subversion.

(C) TECHNOLOGY - CORRUPTION

Altering of data or programs due to viruses, hardware or software failure or power failure.

(D) DICTIONARY - COR•RUP•TION (K•-RIP'SH•N)

1. a. The act or process of corrupting.
   b. The state of being corrupt.
2. Decay; rot.
3. Archaic. Something that corrupts.

(E) GENERAL ENGLISH DICTIONARY

Corrumpable

corrupt

corrupted

corruptedly

Corrupter

Corruptful

corruptibility
corruptible
corrupting
CorruptinglyCorruption of blood
corruptionist
corruptive
Corruptless
corruptly
corruptness
Corruptress
Corsac
corsage
corsair

TRANSLATIONS FOR CORRUPTION

Nederland's (Dutch)
corruptive, verbastering, verloedering
Français (French)
corruption, altération
Deutsch (German)
n. - korruption, Bestechung, Korrumpierung, Fäulnis
ÅëëçíéêÞ (Greek)
n. öèïñÜ, óÞøç, ðáñáöèïñÜ, (ìôö.) äéáöèïñÜ, åîá÷ñåßùóç
Italiano (Italian)
corruzione, alterazione
Português (Portuguese)
n. - corrupção (f)
Ðóññêèé (Russian)
êîððóïöèÿ, ðàçëîæåíèå
Español (Spanish)

n. - corrupción, decadencia, descenso, degradation, soborno, depravation

Svenska (Swedish)

n. - korruption, mutsystem, fördärvande, sedefördärv, förvrängning, förvanskad form, förruttnelse

PRESENT CONCERN WITH CORRUPTION

"If corruption has been an age-old phenomenon, deep-rooted evil and an universal malady afflicting each and every society in one form or another at one time or another" (Padhay 1986:1), then why there is so much concern at the present time with corruption. The reasons are obvious. Pope of Transparency International provides the *raison d'etre* for this concern."Corruption at the highest levels distorts competition so denying the public access to the competitive marketplace. It induces wrong decisions resulting in: wrong projects, wrong prices, wrong contractors, substandard delivery to recoup overpricing, promotes corruption at lower levels and eroded public confidence in leaders. At lower levels, petty corruptions are damaging because they add to transaction costs, exclude those who cannot pay, foster contempt for public servants amongst public and erode capacity for revenue collection" (Pope, 1996:23).

There are still other reasons as to why now corruption is receiving serious attention. First, "there is a widespread perception that the level and pervasiveness of corruption is not only much greater but may well be increasing" (Harris-White, and White 1996:1). Harris-White and White state that both political and administrative corruption is doggedly entrenched in Sub-Saharan Africa and South Asia and very much part of newly-industrialized countries (NICs) of South East Asia, has touched the very highest levels of political office in many Latin American countries and has quickly reached alarming proportions in the post-communist transitional countries including the former Soviet Union and China (1996:1). Second, developments in the 1980s and 1990s against the backdrop of increasing economic liberalization, third wave of democratization and floating of good governance agenda have heightened expectations that an effective and root-and-branch cure of corruption may be found (Harris-White and White, 1996:2). Third, the coming into prominence of such concepts as decentralization, accountability and transparency, human rights, rule of law and sustainable development have considerably influenced efforts to minimize political and administrative corruption in many countries.

CORRUPTION OF CORRUPTION

Defining corruption is also important in the context of global efforts to reduce its influence in public life. But that is not an easy task. Corruption is a social, legal, economic and political concept enmeshed in ambiguity and consequently encouraging controversy. The ambiguity and controversy result from the fact that a number of competing approaches to understanding corruption is available.

Naturally, definitions of corruption focus on one of several aspects of the phenomenon. Various approaches to corruption can be placed into five groups. These are public-interest-centered, market-centered, public-office-centered, public-opinion-centered and legalistic. Proponents of the public-interest-centered approach believe that corruption is in some way injurious to or destructive of public interest (Rogow and Laswell, 1970:54).

Market-centered enthusiasts suggest that norms governing public office have shifted from a mandatory pricing model to a free-market model, thereby considerably changing the nature of corruption (Tilman, 1970:62-64).

Public-office-centered protagonists stress the fact that misuse by incumbents of public office for private gain is corruption (Theobald, 1990:2).

Those who believe in public-opinion-centered definitions of corruption emphasize the perspectives of public opinion about the conduct of politicians, government and probity of public servants (Leys, 1970:31-37).

Others have suggested looking at corruption purely in terms of legal criteria in view of the problems inherent in determining rules and norms which govern public interest, behaviour and authority (Scott, 1972).

The five approaches, as discussed above, have concentrated on the nature of corruption. Though the approaches throw some light they do not clarify the meaning of corruption to any satisfaction. Now there are four divergent views on the definition of corruption. The definitions have come from moralists, functionalists, social denturists and social constructionist realists. The moralists view "corruption as an immoral and unethical phenomenon that contains a set of moral aberrations from moral standards of society, causing loss of respect for and confidence in duly constituted authority" (Gould, 1991:468).

One of the well-known proponents of this view, Nye, portrays corruption as "a behaviour that deviates from the formal duties of a public role (elective or appointive) because of private-regarding (personal, close family, private clique) wealth or status gains, or violates rules against the exercise of certain types of private-regarding influence" (Nye, 1997:417). But this way of defining corruption suffers from a number of limitations. It tends to individualize a societal phenomenon and attempts to dichotomize as to what is good and what is bad. In the process societal contexts are ignored and the gap between formal norms and the underlying practice-girded norms are not analysed (Caiden and Caiden, 1977).

The functionalists usually look at corruption in terms of the actual function that it plays in socio-economic development. Claims are made by functionalists that corruption flourishes as a substitute for the market system; offers an acceptable alternative to violence; increases public participation in public policy (Leff, 1979; Gould, 1980). Some functionalists believe that political and bureaucratic leaders may see a national interest in actively pursuing or tolerating a certain degree of administrative corruption (Klitgaard, 1988). The major criticisms against functionalists are that they ignore the political significance of deviance and lack any consideration of power, interest and social structure in their analyses and at the same time the whole question of the origins of corruption is not considered (Lo, 1993:3).

The two comparatively recent perspectives, i.e., social censure and social construction reality, view corruption radically differently from the other two approaches, i.e. moralists and functionalists. Both the approaches tend to look at corruption from a broad societal perspective. The proponents of social censure believe that in understanding corruption one should take into consideration the capacity of the state to produce a particular form of social relations and shift the theoretical emphasis to the interplay of law, ideologies and political economy (Lo, 1993:5). On the other hand, social construction reality views corruption as problematic and the actors involved can be studied by relating them to contextual information on their social positions, interests and stakes in the system as well as on the political, economic and social conditions within which they function (Pavorala, 1996:25).

In view of the multitude of approaches and views on corruption it is not easy to agree on an unanimous definition of the term. Two definitions of corruption can prove handy. The shorter definition of corruption includes "abuse of authority, bribery, favouritism, extortion, fraud, patronage, theft, deceit, malfeasance and illegality" (Caiden, 1991a).

The broader definition of corruption refers to "use of one's official position for personal and group gain and that includes unethical actions like bribery, nepotism, patronage, conflict of interest, divided loyalty, influence-peddling, moonlighting, misuse or stealing of government property, selling of favours, receiving kickbacks, embezzlement, fraud, extortion, misappropriation, under- or over-invoicing, court tempering, phony travel and administrative documents and use of regulation as bureaucratic capital (AAPAM, 1991). In conformity with these two definitions of corruption the following definitions of political corruption and administrative corruption are adopted here.

Political corruption is "the behaviour of (elected) public officials which diverges from the formal components - the duties and powers, rights and obligations - of a public role to seek private gain" (Kramer, 1997). Administrative corruption is defined as "the institutionalized personal abuse of public resources by civil servants" (Gould, 1991). In both cases public officials (elected and appointive) can convert public office into private gain in many ways.

(A) IMPORTANT DEFINITIONS OF CORRUPTION

- o Inducement (as of a public official) by improper to violate duty (as by coming a felony) he was held on charges of corruption and racketeering.
- o Destroying someone's honesty or loyalty, undermining moral integrity "Corruption of minor" the big city's subversion of rural innocence.
- o The misuse of public or private position of direct or indirect personal gain.
- o Influence over another person exercised through channels that are not socially accepted.
- o Corruption is influence over decisions that doesn't pass through the public mechanisms for influence.
- o The practice of unlawful or improper use of influence, power and other means. Political offices have been susceptible to corruption throughout history.

LITERATURE SURVEY OF CORRUPTION

This section contains a review of important facets of corruption from both conceptual and comparative perspective. The discussion has follows logically from what has been presented in the introductory section. Here the focus is on a number of important yet interrelated aspects of corruption. So, there remains a possibility of overlap in the discussions that follow in this section.

CAUSES OF CORRUPTION

Corruption is a phenomenon that takes place due to the presence of a number of factors. An understanding of such factors requires, among other things, a kind of general framework for a clearer understanding of the causes of corruption, especially from a broader perspective. Genesis of corruption can be explained by looking at three levels - international, national and individual institutional levels (Goudie and Strange, 1997). Competitiveness of international markets provides multinational companies of various sizes with an incentive to offer bribes to gain an advantage over competitors. At the national level basic development strategy of any government moulds opportunities and incentives for corruption. At the same level three relationships - between the government and the civil service, between the government and the judiciary and between the government and the civil society - also affect the nature and discussions of corruption. Three areas of government activity - customs administration, business regulation and management of foreign aid - act as sources of corruption at the level of individual institutions.

Corruption also results from the presence of a number of factors. These include: rapid economic and social change, strong kinship and ethnic ties, new institutions, overlapping and sometimes conflicting views about what is proper public behaviour, governmental monopoly over economic activities, political softness, widespread poverty and socio-economic inequalities, ignorance, lack of knowledge about individual entitlements, communal bonds, ambivalence towards legitimacy of governmental organizations, asymmetric relationship favouring those in control of state power, economic shortages in which public officials assume extraordinary control over scarce goods and services, greed, patronage and systematic maladministration (Gould and Amar-Reyes, 1985; United Nations, 1990). Most of the above-mentioned factors contributing to corruption can be categorized into "six-fold typology". This typology contains ideological, external, economic, political, socio-cultural and technological variables (Caiden, 1991a).

Some of the major reasons as to why people "collude in different ways, rationalize corrupt practices and tolerate corruption in a large scale" are because of the presence of number of factors. These are: governments act as monopolies in many respects, discretion that government and its monopolistic public agencies enjoy in their decision making and allocate roles, lack of effective accountability in government except in the nominal sense of presenting annual audited accounts and reports to parliament or answering questions in the parliament, citizens have limited information about the rules of the game and the standards of service they can expect from public agencies, and exposure of the average citizen to corruption in the public sector tends to be episodic (Paul, 1997a:1350-1351).

FORMS OF CORRUPTION

Corruption takes many forms. These forms are: acceptance of money and other rewards for awarding contracts, violation of procedures to advance personal interests, kickbacks from developmental programmes or multi-national corporations, pay-offs for legislative support, diversion of public resources for private use, overlooking illegal activities, intervening in the justice process, nepotism, common theft, overpricing, establishing non-existing projects and tax collection and tax assessment frauds (UN, 1990).

These many varieties of corruption can be categorized further in terms of their nature. Corruption can be foreign-sponsored, institutionalized, outcome of political scandal and administrative malfeasance (Caiden, 1988). In foreign-sponsored corruption the main actors are public officials, politicians, representatives of donor and recipient countries. Bureaucratic elites, politicians, businessmen and middlemen are responsible for political scandal. Corruption becomes institutionalized as a result of the support provided by bureaucratic elites, politicians, businessmen and white-collar workers. In administrative malfeasance petty officials and interested individuals play major role. Corruption has been differentiated into three types - collusive, coercive and non-conjunctive (Arora, 1993). In collusive corruption the corrupters themselves are willing and active participants in the process and use of corruption as an instrument for inducing wrong action or inaction on the part of authorities, deriving benefit greater than the costs of corruption on their part. Corruption is forced upon the corrupted by those in the position of power and authority in coercive corruption. In non-conjunctive corruption benefits are obtained at someone else's cost and victims are unaware of their victimization. Five major strategies - mystification, distancing, folklore, colonization and pacification - have been used by the beneficiaries to protect, promote and sustain corruption in diverse contexts (Arora, 1993).

COSTS OF CORRUPTION

Corruption is not cost-neutral. There have been claims that not everything is bad about corruption. Its effects can be positive too. Corruption, among other things, assists in capital formation; fosters entrepreneurial abilities, allows business interest to penetrate bureaucracy and permits the logic of market to insinuate itself into transactions from which public controls exclude it (Theobald, 1990). But overwhelming evidence in recent decades suggests that the impact of corruption has been and continues to be negative on all fronts. Corruption has a negative, deleterious and divesting influence on investment and economic growth, administrative performance and efficiency and political development. Continuance of corruption in a country leads to economic malaise and squandering of public resources, lowers governmental performance, adversely affects general morale in the public service, jeopardizes administrative reform efforts and accountability measures, and perpetuates social and economic inequalities (UN, 1990). Corruption reinforces political instability and underdevelopment (Ouma, 1991). In short, corruption impedes economic growth, stifles entrepreneurialism, misuses scarce national resources, weakens administrative capacity, contributes to serious political decay and undermines stability, democracy and national integration (Theobald, 1990).

CHECKING CORRUPTION

Checking corruption is no easy task. Still no one denies the need to check corruption effectively. It may not be possible to eradicate corruption completely but then vigorous and determined actions will go a long way to minimize it. The measures suggested are too many and defy any easy characterization. To contain and minimize corruption a number of measures have been recommended. These include: driving out corruption by means of usually one-off purges or campaigns, setting up of anti-corruption boards, commissions and the like, campaign for moral regeneration or moral re-armament, strengthening of checks on abuse of power and the enhancement of accountability of the powerful as well as public officials, ensuring transparency and openness in governmental activities, develop positive social attitudes, enforcing a code of public ethics, supporting the role of media, improving educational procedures (Theobald, 1990; UN, 1990).

To reduce corruption drastically, a number of fundamental changes must be brought about. These include: reducing the opportunities for corrupt transactions by cutting back the state's activities; emergence of new centers of power outside the bureaucracy; development of competitive party politics; ascendance of universalistic norms; effectuation of far-reaching administrative reform measures affecting policy, institutional and process levels; strengthening of preventive structures and tightening of prosecuting techniques (Theobald, 1990; UN, 1990). What is important about checking corruption is that to be successful one must take into consideration both short-term and long-term views combating corruption.

EXPERIENCES OF COUNTRIES

The experiences of a number of countries pertaining to corruption are reviewed in this sub-section. Cross-country survey covers nature, scope, type of corruption as well as the measures taken to curb corruption and outcome of such efforts. But it needs to be stated that not all aspects of corruption have been covered in the countries concerned due mostly to the non-availability of information.

In the Philippines the network of corruption in the public sector is rather extensive and covers petty fixers, workers at lower levels of the organizational hierarchy to mid-level officials taking undue advantage of their positions, and extending to the elite whose profit from corruption transactions with government runs into millions of pesos but whose powerful positions render them almost untouchable by the law enforcement agencies (Alfiler, 1979). Six types of corruption in the public sector of the Philippines have been identified (Carino and Guzman, 1979). These are: tong, lagay or arreglo, retainer, favor, individualized and systematic corruption. Anti-graft and investigatory agencies appointed by a number of Philipino Presidents failed to effectively check corruption due to organizational instability, frequent changes in leadership, political pressure in employee recruitment, public apathy and strained relations with other branches and agencies of the government (Alfiler, 1979).

In Uganda corruption is the outcome of self-aggrandizement, of unrealistically low remuneration for public servants and a closed political system (Ouma, 1991). Corruption has resulted in the loss of badly needed revenue and skilled manpower, distorted priorities of public policy and shifted scarce resources away from the public interest (Ouma, 1991). Naturally, distrust among different segment of the society has increased and despondency of the people-at-large has been exacerbated.In Ghana the way corruption has been institutionalized in the government is fascinating. In one ministry bribe money is divided in the following manner: 50% to the minister, 20% to the junior ministers, 10% to go-between, 10% to the secretary of the political party in power and the rest to an open cash fund kept by the minister for expenses like paying informers within the ministry, providing gifts to individual visitors and maintaining attractive women around the office (Vine, 1975). The causes for such widespread political corruption are: traditional contexts and effects of colonialism; the new men who inherited political leadership after independence; and bureaucratic transition from a colonial to an indigenous administrative system. Political corruption took its toll in the form of waste of resources, instability and reduction in the capacity of government (Vine, 1975).

It is now commonly agreed that corruption has vitiated India's public life like a cancer spreading over a human body. All sectors, be they administrative or political or economic, have come under the ever-increasing onslaught of corruption. There are many reasons as to why this has happened. Political actors of all shades including ministers, legislators, office-bearers of political parties, and other political office-holders are involved in corruption (Padhay, 1986). Members of the public bureaucracy are no less corrupt. Measures taken to combat corruption like setting up of inquiry commissions have failed. These commissions' findings have not been taken seriously by successive governments and consequently their recommendations have gathered dust. At the same time, some of the commissions were created with a *mala-fide* and political intent. Corruption control is possible only with the adoption and implementation of four national agenda. They are: reforming the political process, restructuring and reorienting the government machinery, empowering the citizens and creating sustained public pressure for change (Guhan and Paul, 1997). Under each a number of appropriate and timely recommendations are made to cleanse the widespread corruption that exists in India at all levels touching almost each and every governmental institution and their functionaries. Singapore and Hong Kong are two countries whose success in effectively tackling corruption in the public service is well-known.When the People's Action Party (PAP) came to power in June 1959 it found a colonial corrupt bureaucracy in place. The PAP, which is still in power, realized something had to be done to minimize corruption in the Singapore Civil Service (SCS). Over a period of time the PAP government introduced a number of measures to curb corruption.

The then existing Prevention of Corruption Ordinance was amended and replaced with the Prevention of Corruption Act (POCA) to curb opportunities for corruption and to increase the penalty for corrupt behaviour (Quah, 1995:148). At the same time additional powers were given to the Corrupt Practices Investigation Bureau by POCA. It is obvious that Singapore's anti-corruption strategy has been effective because it is designed to remove two major causes of corruption - the incentives and opportunities (Quah, 1989).

Corruption in Hong Kong public service had been well-entrenched. Public officials were known to make money utilizing their positions. But the situation changed drastically with the arrival of a new Governor, Sir Murray MacLehose, in 1973. He established an Independent Commission against Corruption (ICAC). The ICAC under the leadership of a distinguished former public official was given a wide array of powers. The ICAC had the power to arrest people on suspicion, search and seize without a warrant, require information, freeze assets and property and prevent people from leaving the colony (Caiden, 1991b:249). The Commission was assisted in its operations by five advisory committees on Corruption, Operations Review, Prevention, Community Relations and Complaints, drawn from cross-section of the population and reported directly to the Governor (Caiden, 1991b:249). The ICAC was organized into three areas: (a) an operations department to investigate, arrest and help prosecute suspects; (b) a corruption prevention department to restructure government organizations to reduce opportunities for corruption; and (c) a community relations department to change people's attitudes toward corruption (Caiden, 1991b:249).

POLITICAL AND ADMINISTRATIVE CORRUPTION

Corruption has a deep root in the society in this part of the world. A chapter in Kautilya's Arthasastra titled "Detection of what is embezzled by government servants out of state revenue" is so vivid and detail that it resembles largely any meticulously prepared official report of today on modes of corruption and how to control such corruption. Kautilya writing many centuries ago identified forty types of embezzlement committed by public servants (Padhay, 1986). In ancient India corruption was prevalent in administration, judiciary and trade. As indicated earlier corruption in one form or another became an integral part of politico-administrative systems during the Khilji and Tuglaq dynasties. The situation did not change during the rule of Mughals and the British. Many politicians were charged with corruption and debarred from politics after the promulgation of the first martial law in Pakistan in 1958. Many civil servants, some belonging to the elite Civil Service of Pakistan (CSP), were dismissed from their services on corruption changes.

It has been argued by some that Bangladesh society is a highly complex network involving reciprocal favours and obligations, and that as a result payoff is the lifeblood of the country (Maloney, 1986:173). Payoff benefits include money, jobs, luxury gifts, building supplies, overseas travel and the payment of foreign tuition bills, foreign medical bills, overseas hotel and restaurant bills and personal liabilities (Kochanek, 1993:258). The symptoms of patron-client relationship are further reflected by the practice of some businessmen to maintain rest houses and high-class exclusive hostesses to entertain important foreign guests and big bosses (Siddiqui, et al. 1990). Many of these big bosses are no doubt top-ranking politicians and senior civil servants.

POLITICAL CORRUPTION

Using position while in power to grant undue favour and benefit to one's relatives, friends and key supporters is a hall-mark of politics in Bangladesh. All the effective rulers have been accused of either direct or indirect involvement in large-scale corruption. During the rule of Sheikh Mujibur Rahman (Mujib) that lasted little over three-and-a-half years (1972-1975) corruption became a major issue in public discussion. Mujib's tendency to grant political and financial benefit to his close relatives and associates is well-known. Awami League (AL) activists received jobs in nationalized industries, grew rich as smugglers, appropriated Pakistani houses and sold off government permits and licenses to the highest bidders (Kochanek, 1993). Sheikh Abu Naser, Mujib's only brother, and four sisters were believed to have benefited excessively from their ties of kinship with Mujib (Franda, 1982). Some of the nouveaux-riches created through the distribution of patronage by the Mujib government were ring leaders of smuggling operations (Maniruzzaman, 1982). Election-related corruption was prominent during Mujib's rule.

Though General Ziaur Rahman (Zia) was not personally involved in corruption, he is credited with institutionalizing corrupt activities (Franda, 1982). It must be said that he instituted legal actions or sacked some ministers on corruption charges, but these people were calling for decentralization in the internal working of his party, i.e. Bangladesh Nationalist Party (BNP). Local units of BNP became pockets of corruption. Zia's failed initiative of Sawnirvar Gram Sarker as the model of "grassroots democracy" was built on loyalty to his party and patronage distribution. During his time corruption and misuse of power resulted in the wastage of almost 40% of the total resources earmarked for development (Kochanek, 1993). Under Zia presidential, parliamentary and local level elections were to some extent manipulated in favour of his party (Khan and Zafrullah, 1979; Khan 1989a).

General Hossain Mohammad Ershad's (Ershad) government established record levels of venality (Blair, et al., 1992). Ershad's government was primarily based on calculated and selective patronage distribution to a favoured few. In fact, under Ershad corruption prevailed in each and every sector of national life and the forms of corruption included petty corruption, project corruption and programmatic corruption (Kochanek, 1993). Ershad holds the record of totally destroying the credibility of the electoral system of the country. Like Mujib and Zia before him he considered the Election Commission as a normal administrative unit to be used and misused to serve his personal, coterie and party interests. The control of the Election Commission was ensured through the appointment of weak and pliable persons as Chief Election Commissioner and Election Commissioners. Introduction of the upazila system in 1982 not only legitimized and strengthened his rule but at the same time contributed immensely to the spread of corruption to the grassroots and in the process vitiated local development and adversely affected local participation. Politics of patronage and corruption became the order of the day in the delivery of local services. An overwhelming majority (93%) of the respondents in a survey conducted in 1991 and 1992 in two upzilas in the districts of Kurigram and Mymensingh held the view that corruption had increased significantly since the introduction of the upazila system (Siddiquee, 1997). Most respondents in the same survey felt that the upazila council was the nerve centre of corruption, nepotism and patronage networks (Siddiquee, 1997).

The study based on survey indicated how upazila councils in study areas extended their patronage networks by: distributing various construction tenders and work orders to their relatives, friends and political allies; leasing out hats, bazars and jalmahals to their chosen parties; issuing these same people with licenses and permits and selecting the members of their own lobby for various project committees (Siddiquee 1997). During Ershad's time the politics-business nexus in the arena of corruption became rather prominent. He is known to have received a fixed percentage on any deal involving any amount of money. This contributed to the emergence of a class of fabulously rich people without much effort on their part and who had little understanding of business ethics or norms and adversely affected those who wanted to pursue business in the traditional manner. These new rich people also became prominent in politics as members of parliament and cabinet and eventually some of them became leader of different chambers and other bodies, thereby cementing a close link between politics and business premised on corruption and patronage. One of the outcomes of such a development has been increasing criminalization of politics. Individuals with proven tract records as criminals became an indispensable party in this unholy alliance between Ershad and his promotees in business. It needs to be added that both Mujib and Zia were instrumental in making individuals with obscure background millionaires. But the difference between Ershad and Mujib and Zia is that the former transgressed all norms, bent rules and broken regulations in order to excessively profit from all state business transactions while the latter operated within limits of civility.

ADMINISTRATIVE CORRUPTION

Corruption has been and continues to be an integral part of culture. The level of corruption varies depending on how influential a position the particular civil servant holds (Khan, 1997). The civil servants have by and large become accustomed to live a life style far beyond their legal income (Zafarullah, 1987). The citizens have accepted the stark reality that nothing moves without adequately satisfying the concerned civil servant (Khan, 1997).

An opinion survey conducted in 1992 of household heads in Dhaka City found that 68.25% of respondents paid bribes to concerned officials to get services (Aminuzzaman, 1996). The findings of the survey indicated that members of law enforcing agencies, customs and income tax departments were involved in administrative corruption (Aminuzzaman, 1996). Another finding of the survey reaffirmed the commonly held belief that the higher the level of bureaucracy the lower the frequency but higher the amount of bribe; and the lower the level of bureaucracy the higher the frequency but less the amount of bribe (Aminuzzaman, 1996).

The Bangladesh Unnayan Parishad (BUP) only recently conducted an opinion survey of 2197 individuals selected randomly from sixty districts. This survey indicated that 95% of respondents felt that the police department was most corrupt while 82% opined that the secretariat (where most ministries/divisions are located) and the judicial system were most corrupt. In the corruption indicator the customs department came second with 91% of respondents considering its officials extremely corrupt. The officials of the Taxation Department were placed in third position as 90% of the respondents felt they were extremely corrupt (BUP, 1997).

Both the surveys reaffirm the ever-widening horizon of administrative corruption. Another survey of people's opinions at two upazilas in Northern Bangladesh indicated that the then upazila structure was not only controlled by centrally-debuted civil servants posted there but they were involved in misappropriating public funds for their own use (Rahman, 1994). Villagers had to bribe civil servants on a routine basis either to bypass certain access encounters or to speed up the process of service delivery (Rahman, 1994). The surveys as part of three case studies indicated that civil servants' control over massive financial resources without proper accountability and the self-seeking nature of civil servants were major contributing factors to the growth and sustenance of administrative corruption at the local level (Rahman, 1994).

Now one may ask the question as to why such large-scale administrative corruption exists. The reasons for such corruption can be summed up (Khan, 1997). First, civil servants involved in corrupt practices in most cases do not lose their jobs. Very rarely they are dismissed from service on charges pertaining to corruption. Still more rarely they are sent to prison for misusing public funds. They have never been compelled to return to the state their ill-gotten wealth. Second, people have a tendency not only to tolerate corruption but to show admiration to those civil servants who make a fortune through dubious means. The underlying assumption is that it does not matter how one has acquired wealth as long as he has done so. Third, it is easier for a citizen to get quick service because he has already paid the civil servant rather than wait for his turn. Fourth, there is now social acceptance of corruption by public officials. Fifth, barring occasional public procurements, the representatives of the people, i.e. politicians in power, are unwilling to take effective measures to curb corrupt practices in public dealings.

NATURE, FORMS AND CONSEQUENCES OF CORRUPTION

Corruption is all-pervasive in Bangladesh. Though corruption has been a part of our politico-administrative heritage, there is little denying the fact that after independence the tentacles of corruption have engulfed the entire society. So strong and sustained is the influence of corruption that most people have come to accept it as a fait accompli. Not only do citizens have accepted it as a part of their daily life experience but more frighteningly they feel themselves powerless to address the phenomenon at any level (Lewis, 1996). The reason for such helplessness is to the presence of corruption in almost all levels of government (World Bank, 1996). The changeover from an authoritarian to a democratic system of government in the 1990s has not had any effect on the nature and dimensions of corruption. Information obtained from the Finance Division of the Ministry of Finance show that over a period of twenty-two years, i.e. between 1971 and 1993, taka 18,000 crore were lost in the public sector due to misappropriation of public funds and theft (Alam, 1996). But this huge amount of money, which is substantial for a resource-poor and aid-dependent country, is only the tip of the iceberg if one takes into consideration all cases of corruption that have been reported by the Bureau of Anti-Corruption over the same period (Khan, 1997).

A government Task Force Report identified a few years back a number of areas where corruption was likely to manifest itself. These areas include: procurement of goods and services including award of contracts by the government; administration of taxes and prevention of smuggling, disposal, sale and allotment of government property include disinvestment of industries and other commercial units; administration of loans by public financial institutions, outright embezzlement of government fund and all kinds of shop-floor malpractices (Ahmed, 1992).

It is usually known that almost all kinds of corruption perpetuate in politics and administration in Bangladesh. The most common form of corruption is pecuniary bribes (Taslim, 1994). Other forms of corruption are: abuse of authority, nepotism, favoritism, fraud, patronage, theft and deceit. In many cases forms of corruptions are intertwined with their consequences.

As one scholar noted:

"Petty corruption takes many forms. Payments are required simply to obtain an application form or a signature, to secure a copy of an approved sanction, to ensure proper services and billing from telephone, natural gas, electric power and water employees. Project corruption permeates both public and private sector contracting. A substantial commission must be paid to secure large public sector contracts in Bangladesh. Programmatic corruption involves Food for Work and relief programmes" (Kochanek, 1993:259,263).

The consequences of these three forms of corruption included among others: high losses suffered by public-sector utilities; forcing donor countries and agencies to hire lobbyists to clear their projects by bribing officials at different levels and failure of Food for Work and relief programmes to reach their targets due to massive theft and huge misuse of resources (Kochanek, 1993).

Other baneful consequences of corruption on the economy include: siphoning away a large chunk of public resources which could have been productively employed somewhere in the economy; undermining of productivity, efficiency and effectiveness of the government; diminishes efficient mobilization of resources and management of development activities; gains through corruption used either in conspicuous consumption or transferred to foreign bank accounts; generates allocative inefficiency by permitting the least efficient contractor or most costly supplier with the highest ability to bribe; bribes and payoffs instead of expediting decisions and facilitating movement of files encourages civil servants to hold back all papers until some payment is made to them; money gained from bribes becomes a part of the expected income; and over-invoicing and under-invoicing of imports and exports and smuggling increases lead to distortion in investment decisions and to capital flight (Ahmed, 1992). Some other equally damaging consequences of corruption are: undermines public confidence in government; engenders wrong economic choices and constrains government's ability to implement policies; makes the poor pay the price; and threatens government's strategy of private-sector-oriented growth (World Bank 1996a: 66).

A recent report of the United Nations Development Programme (UNDP) titled "Corruption and Good Governance" found that bureaucratic corruption and inefficiency are taking a heavy toll on the Bangladesh economy, causing hundreds of millions of dollars' worth of loss in terms of unrealized investment and income (Mustafa, 1997). The report pointed out: "If Bangladesh were to improve the integrity and efficiency of its bureaucracy, its investment would rise by more than five percentage points and its yearly GDP rate would rise by over half a percentage point" (Mustafa, 1997).

ERADICATING CORRUPTION

Eradication of corruption should be the nation's number-one priority in view of the ever-increasing horizon of political and administrative corruption and its baneful multifarious effects on the society-at-large. It needs to be understood by all that eradication of corruption is only possible if strong political commitment exists. Without strong political commitment, bureaucratic reorientation and a vibrant and effective civil society, checking corruption turns into a very difficult almost impossible task. In the context of Bangladesh only radical and fundamental policy measures initiated and strongly backed by a committed political leadership and supported and implemented by a reoriented bureaucracy and watched and monitored by an organized and vocal civil society can control corruption. Given the presence of three crucial variables - committed political leadership, reoriented bureaucracy and an organized and vocal civil society - other policy measures need to be adopted to effectively contain as well as control corruption. What is proposed below are a number of long-term and short-term policy measures placed in wider socio-political and economic contexts to control corruption.

The public sector employs over a million people in 35 ministries, 50 divisions, 221 departments, 139 directorates and autonomous bodies and 153 state enterprises (World Bank 1996b:57). It may also be added that since independence the number of ministries, departments and public servants has doubled (Khan, 1997). In the context of present reality there is little rationale for maintaining a huge public-sector edifice which contributes to corruption in public dealings. There is now justification for right-sizing the government. Right-sizing of government will, among other things, will discourage creation and maintenance of redundant agencies and units and restrain doling out of public-service jobs as political favours.

Public-sector accountability is weak, fuzzy and tenuous at best. This has resulted in the inability to enforce financial contracts, stop theft in public enterprises and hold officials accountable for improper or delayed judgment (World Bank, 1996a: viii). A number of actions need to taken simultaneously to institutionalize and strengthen accountability to effectively counter corruption. First, a bi-partisan parliamentary task force be established to bolster the standing committees, instituting the practice of questioning ministers and providing members of parliament with adequate office and research facilities and setting up of an office of Ombudsman (World Bank, 1996a:viii). A parliamentary secretariat should be established outside the sphere of civil service and manned by competent personnel recruited separately and controlled by the speaker of the parliament (Khan, 1997). Second, the office of the Comptroller and Auditor General (CAG) must be reorganized and strengthened by enhancing the capacity of the CAG (World Bank, 1996a:ix). Third, the standards of performance of ministries/divisions and their attached agencies should be made known to the citizens (Rahman, et al., 1993:52). Fourth, complaint procedures should be in place in government agencies for wider use of citizens (Khan, 1997). Fifth, monitoring procedures need to be tightened so that the concerned civil servant knows the extent of compliance by his subordinates to relevant orders and directives as well as services provided to citizens. Sixth, units be established in each ministry and division to develop and apply performance criteria and measures and to develop internal performance audit (UNDP, 1993:106).

Transparency in public-sector decision making is totally absent. This absence, in turn, contributes to corruption. Civil servants by and large value secrecy and are totally unwilling to share information about decisions with citizens. Openness and transparency are alien concepts in public bureaucracy in Bangladesh (Khan, 1997). A number of actions have been recommended to ensure transparency and thereby considerably empower citizens and consequently contain corruption (World Bank, 1996a: xii). First, the Official Secrets Act of 1923 and Government Service Conduct Rules of 1979 should be suitably modified. Second, a task-force on public-sector transparency should be estabilished with membership from different professional and occupational groups to suggest measures to enhance transparency. Third, necessary steps should be taken to make all contract evaluation reports public, thereby enabling all bidders to see how evaluations are made. Still other steps should be taken to ensure transparency and reduce corruption (Khan, 1997). Fourth, earning and tax payments of all public officials - elected as well as appointed - should be published each year to enable the people to learn about the assets of public officials. Fifth, interested citizens must be allowed access to relevant files and documents. For this to happen the number of files marked secret and top secret should be drastically reduced. Sixth, civil servants long accustomed to transact public business under the veil of secrecy should be appropriately trained and indoctrinated to bring about necessary changes in their attitudes and work habits.

A number of specific policy measures have been recommended to control corruption in politics and administration (World Bank, 1996a: xii; Rahman, et al., 1993:97 and Khan, 1997). First, a high-powered task force to be established consisting of public officials, parliamentarians and leading citizens to review all relevant issues pertaining to corruption and to suggest a comprehensive eradication programme. Second, an autonomous standing committee to be formed with judges, senior public officials and leading citizens to oversee the activities of the Bureau of Anti-Corruption (BAC) as well as authorize investigation in ministries, corporations and other agencies by a statutory appointed and protected public prosecutor. Third, salary and benefits of civil servants need to be at par with their counterparts in the private sector. Fourth, provision of severe punishment including long stays in jails and confiscation of assets and properties to be instituted for civil servants involved in corruption. Other measures have also been suggested to counter political and administrative corruption (Paul, 1997:288-304). Fifth, a code of conduct should be adopted by the parliament to provide guidelines for the conduct of elected representatives and to take appropriate steps when departures from accepted norms are detected. Sixth, elected representatives must be compensated suitably to enable them to devote their attention only to public welfare and service. Seventh, enactment of a law to regulate the functioning of political parties is needed. This law would require political parties to hold regular organizational elections at different levels; maintain prompt and systematic accounts and submit audited accounts to either the Election Commission or the Comptroller and Auditor General; and comply with income tax regulations and guidelines. Eighth, election expenditure needs to be reduced and closely monitored by a designated body. Ninth, deregulation and debureaucratisation, bounded discretion in decision making, realignment of the government's audit and intelligence are to be encouraged to control corruption. Tenth, existence of free media so that they can investigate and expose corrupt practices. Eleventh, voluntary agencies and religious groups as well as other components of civil society can play significant role in constraining corruption in public dealing.

NAYAR'S CONTRIBUTIONS

1- Undoubtedly the problem of corruption is a cancer for many countries in the world including ours.

2- We all more or less agree to the fact that while politicians/ bureaucrats/officers initiate corruption, we all support corruption in some way or other. Whether its paying bribe to House Tax/ Income Tax/Sales Tax/Excise officers to reduce our tax liabilities or paying bribe to the traffic police to avoid a simple Rs. 100 challan for a mistake you just committed.

3- Complexity of laws is very much responsible for advancing corruption. Much has been talked about making the laws simple, but as the politicians and bureaucrats would be the most effected class that never seems to happen.

4- Our politicians are very poor. And have crossed all the boundaries of dignity and respect to earn money. Most of them are involved in huge scams and acts of corruption; no one seems to put a full stop. All the reports conveying that only 10% of the funds reach the public are never discussed in any of the houses of parliament. I think those manager are better who exploit employees for the ultimate gain of the company. Our politicians, in last 50 years, have never thought about the country and development. Look at the way other countries have grown and where are we. Sounds good when we hear economy growing at 8%, but, shamefully, we still are at the bottom end of the development list. Those countries of Africa and South America, which we talk as tribal countries, are far ahead of India in terms of per capita income. Still the leaders concentrate on accumulating personal wealth for the term they are in power.

5- Good people either never come in politics or have to get corrupted to reach the top. I think this is one area where we all can work. No point just talking about corruption lets fight it out.

6- You go to any other country and observe the same Indians; they would be following all the regulations and rules dedicatedly and religiously. Why not in your own country. Because we know we can get away by laws/police/courts by paying bribes. Ask any lawyer/judge and you would know anything is possible by paying bribes. I don't think I need to comment on policemen.

One of our school teachers used to say that you just need three Cs to achieve anything Courage, Conviction and Confidence and three D's - Determination, Dedication and Discipline. Its good to talk about it like I have done above, but the real crux of the matter is to act in the direction of curing the cancer. Its not only about corruption, its about the way of living. All aspects of life, if you have to stop at the stop line while driving, what encourages us to cross the same by 5 feets and then stop - no corruption involved here, but surely some thing to do with how you want to lead your life. Sandeep Kulkarni truly said that we are all not satisfied by what we have - I would add to that - that we all want to get more by wrong means thinking that we are smarter than others.

THOUGHTS OF IVESTIGATORS

Now, I would like to put forward some of my thoughts on the subject:

1- The root cause of corruption appears to be "Ever growing needs of a common man". To put in other words, "No one is satisfied with what ever he/she has got"; and with the advent of new and newer technologies, i do not think the greed is going to end anywhere. May be, I would call 'corruption' is a by-product of 'evolution'.

2- To eradicate (or even to reduce) the evil, firstly, i was trying to figure out the problem area i.e. whether bribing someone to do some thing, which he/she would not have done other-wise, is the problem after all. To be true, i am still groping in the dark.

3- I believe, there are millions who would not be able to make ends meet, if corruption ceased to exist. For many, there is no choice but to go for it and most of the programmer's of World Bank (and like agencies) are targeted towards increasing the standard of life of those people.

4- Acts of corruption done by a person to sustain his/her life can not be treated a par with Corrupt practices at high places.

5- To reduce the menace of corruption, we may priories our target areas, based on some criterion which should not only include monetary aspect, but also its effect in the society. For eg - Police, Judiciary, Legislature, Corporate etc. Bureaucrats may take lead in this regard, as they have ample power and areas under their jurisdiction to implement clean and transparent governance standards.

6- Completion amongst corporate is another area, which leads to corruption. There, the root cause is not "bare sustenance" but profits, prestige, brand value etc. Thanks to some big corporate, better standards corporate governance have at least started in our economy. I hope others will take a cue from them and follow the policy of "Be good do good".

7- World Bank sources say that the cost of corruption is around $ 1 Trillion. I hope, it is the amount which goes into circulation without being accounted/audited/taxed etc. (Black Money). But after all, that money is also public money and is being circulated amongst them, and put for their use. Even if it would have been accounted/ taxed, it was supposed to be utilized for socio-economic development of the public.

Take for example if a person/corporate has X amount of black money, he will try to derive most profit out of it. Many of the real estate purchases involve flow of black money, and the real estate so formed give profits as well as asset for its owner.The underlying point is that if a person/corporate executes all his liabilities towards the government by way of taxes etc. his money is not put for efficient use. Rather, he can use that more efficiently. I believe, the inference is that the management of public money is not being done properly (that puts a question mark on faith of a person/ corporate in government).

8- Hence, it is more or less up to public representatives, bureaucrats and how they manage public money that the level of corruption in an economy is dependent upon. We need more and more competitive & sincere people at the topmost level. Lastly, I would further like to say that apart from making contributions in this forum, if we could impress/ push for better governance in some form, it would be more practical approach, and who can be a better person than yourself to lead such a thing.

CONCLUSION

Corruption is a complex multi-faceted social phenomenon with innumerable manifestations. It takes place as an outcome of deficiencies in the existing public administration apparatuses and systems as well as cultural, economic, political and social factors.Differences of opinion still exist as to the meaning of the term corruption. This is primarily because individuals look at corruption from their own vantage points influenced by surrounding environment. But what is heartening is that in recent years corruption is viewed from a much broader perspective rather than looking at it from moral and functional angles only.The causes of corruption are as varied as the phenomenon itself. Corruption results from the presence of a number of factors. Typologies have been offered to make a sense out of so many contributory factors.

There are many forms of corruption. To understand the dynamics of so many types of corruption attempts have been made to classify different forms of corruption into broad categories. What transpires from such a categorization is that corruption can be sponsored by outsiders, resultant of political scandal, institutionalized and administrative malfeasance. The cost of corruption has been enormous in terms of a country's socio-political and economic advancement. What has been conclusively demonstrated is that corruption has negative consequences on economic growth, administrative efficiency and political development. Checking corruption is a crying need of today's world. At the same time, it is understood that total eradication of corruption is not possible. But that does not mean in any way that corruption cannot be effectively contained. A number of recommendations have been offered as how to check corruption in a decisive manner. But what has been realized is that in order to drastically reduce corruption fundamental changes must be brought about without any delay or hesitation.

Experiences of the Philippines, Uganda, Ghana and India have clearly indicated that corruption networks are extensive and cover within their realms public servants of all types. What is more alarming is that a rather cozy nexus exists among public servants and politicians in power to share the booties of corruption. Almost all efforts to contain corruption in these countries have been unsuccessful. On the other hand, experiences of Hong Kong and Singapore demonstrate in no uncertain terms that given political will and the institution of appropriate anti-corruption mechanisms incidence of corruption can be drastically contained. The root of corruption in Bangladesh runs deep in history. The existence of a patron-client relationship reinforces corrupt practices in all spheres of public dealing. Almost all political regimes in Bangladesh have been corrupt. Only the nature and extent of corruption varied depending on the nature of the regime, its key leader and his popular power base.

Corruption in the public service is extensive and all-pervasive. Corruption in the political arena has emboldened public servants to become unabashedly corrupt and not bother about it at all. The prevalence of systematic corruption in Bangladesh society can be explained due to a number of factors. Lack of political will, lack of organized movement by civil society for a change in the status quo, and presence of a change-resistant institutional bureaucracy, lack of ethics in public life, absence of independence of judiciary and media, have all contributed in varying degrees to the continuance of large-scale and systematic corruption in all spheres of Bangladeshi society.

2

A Brief Review of Related Literature

Review of related literature is an important prerequisite to actual planning and then the execution of any research work. Familiarity with the literature in any problem helps the investigator to discover what is already known, what others have attempted to fine out, what methods can be promoting and disappointing and what problems remain to be solved. The review of related literature enriches the investigator and directs him to go deep in the investigation. The study of related literature helps in acquiring information about the study done in the field, protects against unnecessary duplication, guides in carrying out the investigation successfully and makes him families with the steps. The existing researches that are directly or indirectly related to present study may be conveniently classified under these broad categories.

Due to rich tradition of philosophical thought, a substantial research must be done in philosophical thought of education. But researchers have not sufficiently focused their attention on value oriented education and philosophical thought of education. Even those studies on value oriented education carried out in India have been isolated, fragmentary and do not contribute much qualitatively to arrive at meaningful and comprehensive conclusions. Here an attempt was made to study the attitudes of engineering students towards value oriented education. The literature to the present problem is described under sub-heads of

- Studies related to Meaning, Definition and Current situation of Corruption.
- Studies related to Women role in Good Governing.
- Studies related to Women role in fighting against Corruption.
- Studies related to Education-Corruption.
- Studies related to Commissions and Committees towards Corruption.
- Studies related to Teachers and Parents role towards Corruption.
- Studies related to Survey towards Corruption.
- Studies related to Causes of Corruption.
- Studies related to Corruption Rally.

STUDIES RELATED TO MEANING, DEFINITION AND CURRENT SITUATION OF CORRUPTION

- **CORRUPTION: noun**

1. Dishonest or illegal behaviour, especially of people in authority.
2. The act or effects of making somebody change from moral to immoral standards of behaviour.
3. The form of a word or phrase that has become changed forms its original form in some way.

Definition: An act done with intent to give some advantage inconsistent with official duty and the fights of others. It includes bribery; but is more comprehensive, because an act may be corruptly done, through the advantages to be derived from it be not offered by another.

Some times corruption is understood as something against law, such as, a contract by which the borrower agreed to pay the lender usurious interest. It is said, in such case that it was corruptly agreed.

1. **Word reference.com:** Lack of integrity or honesty (especially susceptibility to bribery) use of a position of trust for dishonest gain.

Global Corruption Report: Global Corruption Report focuses on the need for greater access to information in the struggle against corruption. Covering worldwide corruption from July 2002 to 2003.

Transparency International: Transparency international is the leading global non-governmental organization devoted to combating corruption. Its mission is to create change towards a world free of corruption.

December 9 2004 An International Anti-Corruption day.

CURRENT SITUATION

- The integrity of the state's authority is very important to people.
- The population is dissatisfied with the irresponsible use of state authority and their representatives who have permitted corruption to prosper.
- Non-Governmental Organization (NGOs) and media are focusing attention on the problem of corruption.
- The political parties support the development of an anti-corruption policy.
- Sufficient information is available to build a successful anti-corruption bureau has been created to play a central role in preventing and combating corruption.
- Legislation is being enacted but its implementation is often delayed.
- International organizations insist on the prevention and combating of corruption and offer assistance.
- There fore the people and the government must demonstrate a true, common, natural will to prevent and fight corruption.

STUDIES RELATED TO WOMEN ROLE IN GOOD GOVERNENCE

Women justify reservation policy in panchayats.

Bharat Dogra portrays Indian women leaders in local governments.

In 1993 one of the most important step for the empowerment of women and increasing their participation in decision making was taken by reserving 33% seats for women in panchayat raj institutions. This paved the way for election of around one million at the village, block and district level. By now most states with a few exceptions like Bihar have completed at least one five year term. What has been the experience of around 7 to 8 lakh women during their first tenure? What lessons can be learnt for the future from this experience?

Given the chance, they excel:

It is easy to point out numerous examples of women who have worked entirely according to what they were told by their husbands or other male members of their families. In some cases elected women remained at home while their husbands attended the panchayat meetings and carried out official transactions on their behalf. Some of the elected women were approached by men only when their signatures (or thumb impressions) were needed. All this is true to a substantial extent, but this is not the whole picture. In our male dominated society it is easy to hear jokes about the subservient role of several elected women, and some fierce arguments based on that reservation for women has failed. Nothing could be further from the truth. In order to realize the greater potential created by these reservations, we should look at several other examples in which women got an opportunity to play an independent role. In such situations time and again, we see them making remarkable achievements for development of their village and quite often resisting the presence of vested interests with a lot of grit and determination.

They bring new perspectives:

The yearnings of several women to assert their independence and make a significant contribution to the welfare of the people are visible in many such examples. In many cases they have been helped by volunteer organizations and people's movements active in their region. In some cases enlightened family members, including husbands, have also encouraged them to realize their potential of initiating meaningful social change. From such examples it is quite clear that when the conducive conditions exist for women to play a leading and active role in the decision making of the village, the entire village community benefits. This increased participation of women is often associated with better utilization of financial resources, increased harmony in village and prioritization of some important but neglected aspects of development such as girls' education and sanitation. Social reform measures such as reduction in alcohol consumption and domestic violence clearly get more prominence when women come to the forefront in rural communities.

Corruption has been one of the main problems of panchayat raj institutions. Interviews in several villages confirm that when women representatives function in an independent way, possibilities for corruption are lesser. Even if a pradhan or sarpanch is honest, there is the other threat that government officials refuse to release money and do not cooperate in other ways unless a certain commission is paid to them. There have been numerous examples of women sarpanchs resisting these demands of officials. In fact one hears of such resistance from women more frequently than from men. This opposition to the demand for commission has been strongly voiced by several women pradhans at their open meetings and training programmes.

Specific cases

Pushpa Rana, pradhan of Arakfarm panchayat in Dehradun district strongly resisted the bribe demands of officials. Although this created a lot of delays and other problems, she finally had her way. Sojar Bai of Ramtek panchayat [district Harda in Madhya Pradesh] went one step further and got the corrupt official [who demanded a cut from her] suspended from his job.

As for the careful use of scarce funds, Alka Chauhan provided a lesson to government engineers. A support wall that had been built in her village Nalapani [district Dehradun] at a cost of Rs. 42,000 had collapsed. A junior government engineer estimated that it will cost Rs.45,000 to rebuild the wall. But Alka Chauhan mobilised the villagers to build the wall at a cost of only Rs.23,500 and the money saved in this way could be spent on other development work. When Suraiya Begum became the chairperson of Sultanpur Chilkana Nagar panchayat, it was saddled with debts and even some of her supporters feared that new development work may be hindered by the need to first clear old debts. But she managed the situation in such a way that by the time she completed her first five year tenure, a record number of development works worth Rs.80 lakhs had been completed.

More women leaders

As Rehana, a social worker of Sultanpur says, "Women are known to use money very carefully at home and somehow manage the family budget even when income is low. Women show the same abilities when they manage the village funds." Her colleague Shaheen adds, "When men are in-charge of development works, they indulge in a lot of wasteful spending in inaugurations and completion ceremonies. Women know how to be frugal and concentrate on the real work." Women representatives have shown the capacity to increase the panchayat income to make the development work more self-reliant. Many elected women have been closely involved with the promotion of self-help groups in villages. Urmila Yadav, sarpanch from Kosli village [Haryana] first took a step to clear encroachments on panchayat land and then built some shops on it. The rent from these shops can provide a regular income to the panchayat.

Women are generally known to have a greater capacity for resolving disputes. When she was the chairperson Suraiya Begum's door always remained open for many victims domestic violence. She helped to resolve many disputes. Pushpa Rana prevailed upon villagers to first settle all disputes locally and go to the police only if village level efforts failed. The result was that the money people had to spend on paying bribes to the police and middlemen was saved. Many elected women representatives have made an effort to reduce liquor consumption and to remove liquor vends. In Ghazidipur village of Saharanpur district, a panchayat member Kamia confronted the pradhan who supported the location of a liquor vend in the village and successfully mobilised village women for the removal of this liquor vend. Veena Sajwan, who was elected block pradhan of Bhilangana block [Tehri Garhwal district] at the young age of only 23 says, "I have taken up anti-liquor issue as the most important issue to mobilise women. When I had the opportunity to meet the Chief Minister, I immediately reminded him of his promise to curb the liquor menace." All over Uttaranchal state this has been an important issue for elected women and they raised it vociferously at a recent 'Open Forum' meeting in Almora.

Battling the male empire

It is hoped that greater participation of women will result in better implementation of water, sanitation, girls education, women's health and maternity. Chandravati Singh made a detailed survey of where exactly hand pumps were needed in her panchayat. [Garchapa in Chitrakut district, UP] which is spread over a wide area. This led to maximising benefits from the limited budget at her disposal for drinking water schemes. Some women elected members have prioritised toilets for ladies at bus stops, a clear need which had been ignored earlier by men pradhans.

In Sirmaul panchayat of Indore district, the sarpanch Kiran Kanchal not only set up a maternity home but also set up a committee to run it on a viable basis without raising the service charges too high for villagers. Madhu Semval [Nathuvala panchayat, Dehradun district] helped to check the spread of a cholera epidemic. Natho Begum [pradhan of Enfield gram panchayat, Dehradun district] was so devoted to promoting the education of girls that she donated her own land for this purpose, even though she herself belongs to a poor family. Some women have overcome heavy odds to accomplish very commendable work in panchayats. Sudha Patel [sarpanch of Changa village, Anand district of Gujarat] is blind, but her work with the help of a friend has won widespread praise. Rajjo, a Dalit woman is completely illiterate and comes from a very poor family. However her work in Sultanpur Chilkana as deputy chairman was so good that almost the entire village adores her.

Some women have resisted efforts of vested interests to harass and dislodge them with a lot of courage and firmness. So many efforts were made to dislodge Ramali Behn from Ahmedabad zila panchayat by powerful vested interests, but she survived them all by her transparent way of functioning and by establishing direct relationship with people. When efforts were made to implicate Savita Behn Bharat Singh Pasaya [sarpanch of Pandra, Dohod district, Gujarat] and her family members in false allegations, she proved her innocence before a large gathering of villagers and officials.

All round progress

When women succeed in overcoming heavy odds to achieve good results in panchayats and also face vested interests with courage, it has an exemplary impact on a large number of other women. They also want to come forward to participate more actively in village affairs and contribute to the welfare of the community. Apart from this, it is also quite evident from the examples given above that the more active role of women in village often contributes to the welfare of the entire community and several important areas which were neglected earlier, now get prioritised. Thus it is in the interests of not just women but the entire village community to encourage the further empowerment of women in village affairs. The 33% reservation for women in panchayat raj institutions is an important part of this empowerment of women. To further strengthen the effort of elected women representatives, the government should provide greater security to women from the anger of powerful vested interests who try to harm and harass them in various ways. Voluntary organisations should also play a crucial role in helping and training elected women representatives.

STUDIES RELATED TO WOMEN ROLE IN FIGHTING AGAINST CORRUPTION

Addis Ababa, July 01, 2003 (WIC) State Minister of Finance and Economic Cooperation, Dr. Mulu Ketsela said Women's active involvement in the fight against corruption was crucial. Speaking at an awareness raising workshop organized for women representing all the regional states under the theme "women's role in the anti-corruption struggle", Dr. Mulu Ketsela said because women represent the most vulnerable half of the society, the enhancement of their participation in combating corruption would have a tremendous impact on the over all program underway across the nation.

Due to various cultural and social factors posed against them, women are the prime victims of poverty Dr. Mulu said adding that corruption has compounded the challenges to their lives. She said studies have repeatedly disclosed that females are more responsible and are more adherent to ethical standards in their positions than are men, and their participation in fighting this social malpractice is therefore essential. Dr. Mulu added that women's natural and social responsibility in raising children and building a society will make easier the effort to create ethical and corruption-free society in the country.

She therefore, underscored the importance of scaling up the awareness level of women about the impacts of corruption and the need for ethics so that they can play their share in alleviating the problem. Public Relations Counselor with the Commission Birhanu Asseffa said on the occasion that the Commission has realized from the outset that without the empowerment of women the anti-corruption program launched in the country would not be successful.

The workshop was therefore organized with the view of making them aware of the prevailing problem of corruption in the country and the means of tackling it, Birhanu said. Participants are expected to replicate the knowledge they have obtained among their respective organizations, he said. Taking part in the two-day workshop are 60 participants representing Community Based

Organizations (CBOs) in all regional States non-governmental organizations working on women and children, and civic societies.

STUDIES RELATED TO EDUCATION-CORRUPTION

Corruption in all of its many forms has become a central issue in higher education worldwide. Rapid expansion, fueled by growing demand for access; dramatic increase in private higher education providers; the marketization of many aspects of higher education; and the financial problems faced by institutions and teaching and administrative staff have all contributed to a variety of corrupt practices. Academic corruption can be found in all countries but is especially prevalent in countries facing severe economic hardships and resultant pressure on their higher education systems, in systems with little external supervision and inadequate quality assurance mechanisms, and in countries in which there is a good deal of societal corruption.

Because of its tradition of probity and reliance on objective and meritocratic values, the problem of corruption is especially important for higher education. Academic institutions and the professoriate claim a special status in all societies—the right to academic freedom and individual and institutional autonomy and a high social prestige. Universities, after all, are responsible for educating the next generation of leaders, conducting scholarly research, and providing objective social analysis. As the national competitiveness in the global economy comes to increasingly depend on the quality of knowledge generated within and on the quality of education provided by a country's higher education institutions, the costs of academic corruption become considerable.

The dictionary definition of corruption will suffice for academe: "impairment of integrity, virtue, or moral principle; inducement to wrong by improper or unlawful means." Corruption in higher education can occur at both institutional and systemic levels and influences university examinations, the conferring of academic credentials, the procurement of goods and services, academic and administrative staff recruitment and promotion, budget allocation and utilization, property management, and the licensing and accreditation of institutions. Instances of academic corruption may involve bribery, facilitation of cheating and impersonation, the establishment of diploma mills, forgery and falsification of examination results, degrees and credentials, patronage, cronyism, and professional misconduct among teachers.

The primary goal of the Higher Education Corruption Monitor is to shed light on corrupt practices of all kinds in different countries, provide resources on current research on corruption in higher education, and serve as a forum for information exchange. The Monitor will collect and, in some cases, summarize news reports, documents, legal testimony, university reports, conference materials, research articles, and other kinds of documentation, and make the data available through a dedicated website. The Monitor will also collect information on policies and initiatives of international agencies and on various measures and reforms undertaken in different countries to address the challenges of corruption in higher education. The Monitor will link its website with websites of other institutions and agencies interested in the topic and with other on-line resources on corruption in order to avoid duplication and at the same time provide maximum attention to the issue. From time to time, the Monitor may issue reports on specific themes relating to corruption in higher education. The Monitor will not seek to verify each item placed on its website but will make every effort to choose reputable reports. The website will be part of the Center for International Higher Education's widely used website.The Monitor will be coordinated by Natia Janashia, graduate assistant in the Center for Higher Education.

A complete whole, connecting them by notes and explanations, where these were necessary; not putting the history in his own words or presenting it from his own standpoint as a modern historian would do, but piecing together the sections of the sources which referred to the same events, and thus preserving not only the history, but the very words in which it had reached him, for all coming generations. In this writer's work we have the Pentateuch of the OT Scriptures.

Geddes MacGregor has afforded, inter alia, another type of corruption in his esteemed book 'The Bible in the Making'. It would be pertinent to give an excerpt from it as well. For all the care that scribes often devoted to their task, a great many errors inevitably crept in. Deviations occur even among the most reliable of the ancient Greek manuscripts.

Before the invention of printing, the difficulty of reproducing the Bible did not consist solely in the labour of copying by hand. Parchment was scarce, so that contractions were very freely used. Sometimes a valuable manuscript, such as the Codex Ephraim, a fifth-century Bible now in the Bibliophile National, Paris, was treated so that, the writings have been erased by scraping and pumicing, the pages might be used over again for making another book. The lower writing was not usually quite obliterated, however, though it was extremely difficult to decipher it until chemical means were found to revive what had been rubbed out. Such a book, with one set of writing superimposed upon another, is called a palimpsest [stress added]. Again, MSS were often corrected by later copyist who scraped out with a knife what seemed to them incorrect, and modern scholars know that in many cases it was the corrector, not the MS, that was at fault. Sometimes a note would be made in the margin which a subsequent copyist would take to be part of the text. The hazards of inaccuracy in copying out the Bible by hand in the circumstances that prevailed in those days were so great that it is indeed astonishing that a text has been preserved which, despite technical problems it presents to the learned, may be taken as generally not straying very far from the sense of the original.

Point-wise recapitulation summaries have been afforded for some of the early parts of this article. They cover almost all of the important points. Thereafter, it was not deemed necessary. It was also not considered proper to quote more authorities. All the important themes have been elucidated. Moreover, almost all of the real and unbiased authorities unanimously endorse these themes. It can safely be concluded on the basis of the above evidence that the text of the OT of the Bible, verbatim et literatim, cannot be taken as free from corruption and alteration. However, the real message can be collected from it, using the critical and analytical apparatus. It may be noted that these types of corruption crept into the text of the Bible in spite of all the humanly possible care that had been sincerely afforded by the early scholars of the Bible. Geddes MacGregor has noted some measures taken towards the faultless transmission of the Bible texts. He notes... With the fall of the Temple at Jerusalem in that year [A.D. 70], the ritual worship with its animal sacrifices was at end, and the dispersed Jews had nothing to take with them on their wanderings but their Bibles. To the copying out of these they devoted immense care. The regulations for making a copy of the Scriptures are set forth in the Talmud (the great post-Biblical collection of Jewish law and legend) and show how scrupulously careful the scribes had to be. The scroll of the Law for use in a synagogue had to be fastened, for instance, with strings made from the skin of 'clean' animals. The length of each column was prescribed: not more than sixty nor fewer than forty-eight lines were permitted. Lines had to be drawn before the writing was done, and if a scribe inadvertently wrote more than three words without first lining his copy, the whole thing was rendered worthless. He had to see that the space of a thread lay between each two consecutive letters that he wrote, and he was not allowed to write even a single letter from memory, without first looking at the approved text from which he was making the copy. He had to see that he never began the sacred name of God with a pen newly dipped in ink, lest he spatter this. The ink had to be black, made exactly according to a carefully delineated prescription. Throughout the whole of his work, the scribe was required to sit in full Jewish dress, and he was forbidden to speak to anyone, even a king. Any copies that did not entirely conform to the exacting standard had to be destroyed. What chiefly accounts for the absence of early Hebrew MSS, however, is the fact that as soon as any scroll became worn out it had to be put in a special room called Geniza, adjoining the synagogue, the contents of which room were periodically cleared out and destroyed. The Jews had no interest in preserving tattered old copies of the Scriptures for the sake of their antiquity: what they wanted were accurate copies, and so long as accuracy of current copies was ensured by the rigid regulations, old ones could be discarded.

It can thus be safely concluded that the text of the OT had to suffer many a type of setback due to a number of reasons as detailed above. As such all possible analytical and critical measures should be adopted to ascertain the validity and intent of its text. But, at the same time, withal its shortcomings, it has preserved a lot of theological, historical, and prophetic substance in it and is not to be discarded outright.

STUDIES RELATED TO COMMISSIONS AND COMMITTEES

National anticorruption agencies, which could be a vital force in preventing corruption, are frequently so politicized that they are ineffective. In this article, two officials of Transparency International discuss how anticorruption agencies can become key players in the war against bribery.

Most development institutions today are promoting good governance in an effort to ensure the success of the projects they are helping to finance. Their focus is on curbing corruption among government officials—the abuse of public office for private gain. But the challenges of preventing and curbing corruption are, if anything, becoming more complex. Transparency International's experiences and those of its national chapters leave little doubt that the rising number of anticorruption initiatives being developed are running up against a massive wall of corrupt practices.

Transparency International's Corruption Perception Index and Bribe Payers Index show that bribe taking in many developing and transition countries is extensive, primarily because of low public sector salaries, senior public officials' and politicians' de facto immunity from prosecution, and greed. Meanwhile, trans-national corporations' propensity to pay bribes is considerable. To be effective, ant bribery initiatives must recognize and confront these realities.

Although national anticorruption agencies can be critical in preventing corruption before it becomes rampant, not only are they difficult to set up but they often fail to achieve their goals once they have been established. They may be so beholden to their political masters that they dare not investigate even the most corrupt government officials; they may lack the power to prosecute; and they may be poorly staffed. One key to success in building effective anticorruption agencies rests in the willingness of the proponents of good governance to share their experiences and to work together to develop greater knowledge of best practices. Our experience suggests that international organizations can make a major contribution on this front, but only if they work in partnership with national authorities and civil society, which, in turn, need to embrace business, academia, and a broad range of nongovernmental organizations. This can happen only when the organizations themselves approach the challenge with a fresh and open mind.

If major anticorruption initiatives are to be firmly anchored, there need to be distinct national government agencies dedicated to curbing corruption. These agencies must command public respect and be credible, transparent, and fearless. They must be subject to review by a free press and by civil society—indeed, they must be accountable to the public. But they must also be given considerable political independence so that they cannot be removed at the whim of enraged political elite.

A prime challenge in many countries is to mobilize the necessary political will to establish such agencies. The World Bank, the IMF, and bilateral aid agencies may call upon governments to establish anticorruption agencies as components of good governance programs and may even make loans conditional on the establishment of such agencies. But these agencies are not likely to succeed unless they are strong enough and politically independent enough to win the public's respect. Reforms therefore need to be firmly grounded within a particular country and not imposed from the outside.

New public procurement approaches

Anticorruption agencies need to focus on public procurement, which gives rise to some of the most egregious abuses. A recent survey in leading emerging market countries that was commissioned by Transparency International and carried out by Gallup International found that public works and construction are widely perceived to be the sectors most riddled by corruption, followed by the defense sector. On a scale of 0 to 10, with 10 being corruption free, the perceived level of corruption in public works and construction was 1.5, while defense

Recently, Transparency International started to work with the government of Nigeria to devise ways of tackling corruption in public procurement. Drawing on the experience of New York City, where efforts to drive organized crime out of the school-construction industry have been successful, a working group established by the Nigerian government determined that bidders should be required to disclose all commissions by affidavit and on oath and that the names of all agencies involved in procurement proceedings should be published. Further, contracts should state that a substantial percentage of the purchase price will be forfeited to the government as liquidated damages should there be any breach. By focusing on changing the way contracts are written, the government was able to avoid the legislative battles that would have occurred had it tried to get new procurement rules passed by parliament, while ensuring that the new requirements were clearly stated in bidding documents.

Transparency International

Transparency International, founded in 1993, is a not-for-profit, nongovernmental organization dedicated to curbing corruption. Its headquarters are in Berlin. National chapters of Transparency International exist, or are being developed, in more than 70 countries. The organization works to strengthen civil society leadership and to forge coalitions—led by civil society and embracing business, government, and academia—in efforts to curb corruption. Transparency International has participated actively in building international support for the Organization for Economic Cooperation and Development's Anti-Corruption Convention, which came into force in February 1999, and other legislative actions to criminalize the payment of bribes. At the same time, Transparency International works to stimulate the development and expansion of anticorruption programs by national governments and international organizations and to build a base of knowledge and best practices that can be widely used in these efforts. Transparency International's research and its national integrity source book, working papers, and overall information base can be found on its website, http://www.transparency.org.

Hong Kong SAR as a model

Nigeria has a long way to go, but it can be encouraged by examples of effective approaches in other countries. National anticorruption agencies, for example, can go far beyond merely identifying and prosecuting corrupt officials, vital as this is. They can also assist in creating an environment in which large public works proceed without corruption. They can operate in ways that command the respect of contractors and contribute to the building of a business environment that is imbued with integrity. Although these aspirations sound utopian, they can be realized, as Hong Kong SAR has demonstrated.

Michael Wiehen and Peter Rooke, members of Transparency International's Board of Directors, recently examined the procurement processes involved in developing Hong Kong SAR's Airport Core Program (ACP), which included construction of the Hong Kong airport, as well as of high-speed rail and road connections, a major suspension bridge, and a cross-harbor tunnel. The total capital cost of the ACP exceeded HK$160 billion (US$20.6 billion at the current exchange rate of US$1 = HK$7.75), making it one of the largest infrastructure projects ever undertaken anywhere in the world. The ACP was virtually free of corruption, owing to several factors:

- Hong Kong SAR's clear, strict Prevention of Bribery Ordinance and strong Independent Commission Against Corruption (ICAC), which has impressive legal powers and a staff of about 1,350 professionals;

- clear rules and effective control mechanisms for selecting and procuring consultant and construction services and equipment supplies, supervising and monitoring the implementation of contracts, enforcing the accountability of government staff as well as of consultants and contractors, and resolving disputes;
- the establishment, for ACP purposes, of special institutions such as the New Airport Projects Coordinating Office (since dissolved), which had a dispute-resolution team that stepped in whenever problems occurred, and the Engineering and Associated Consultant Selection Board, which is also involved in non-ACP projects; and
- a favorable working environment, including appropriate salaries for civil servants, a high degree of professionalism and pride among the officials, and a relatively small society in which businessmen caught offering bribes or otherwise trying to manipulate the processes find it difficult to obtain other business, making corruption a high-risk activity.

The ICAC has been pivotal to the success of transparent public procurement in Hong Kong SAR. Its work is carried out by three departments. The Operations Department carries out the investigation and prosecution of offenses; the Corruption Prevention Department examines the practices and procedures of government departments and public bodies and makes recommendations on how opportunities for corruption can be eliminated or reduced; and the Community Relations Department is responsible for educating the general public about the evils of corruption, instilling positive values in Hong Kong's youth—starting as early as kindergarten—providing advice to business organizations on drawing up codes of conduct, and harnessing support for the ICAC.

Other successful anticorruption agencies are found in Australia, Botswana, Malawi, Singapore, and South Africa (under the post-apartheid government). However, most countries are just starting to think about setting up anticorruption agencies, so there is an urgent need to establish clear guidelines of best practice.

Guidelines

The starting point should be identifying the core role of anticorruption agencies. Given that prevention is always better than prosecution, a small investigative and monitoring unit with appropriate authority and political independence may be much better placed than other government agencies to ensure that effective preventive steps are identified and taken. Research by Transparency International suggests that to operate successfully, an anticorruption agency must have the following:

- Political support not only from a country's president but also from a broad array of national political leadership.
- Tthe political and operational independence needed to investigate the highest levels of government (some agencies that have failed—for example, those in Tanzania and Zambia—are housed within the president's office and therefore have scant opportunity to tackle corruption involving the national political leadership);.
- Access to documentation and the power to question witnesses; and
- Leadership with great integrity.

Further, credibility and effectiveness depend on the exemplary behavior of the anticorruption agency itself. It must act, and be seen to act, in conformity with international human rights norms. It must operate under the law and be accountable to the courts.

A test for a government establishing an anticorruption agency is whether it would find the agency's actions acceptable if it were the political opposition rather than the party in power. An enduring formula, which seems fair and workable to everyone, whether in or out of government, needs to be found. This requires, for example, that the agency have significant powers of investigation, prosecution, and deterrence, independent of political parties and government leaders. Accountability is critical to the agency's success, as are checks on its power and the method used for selecting its leadership. Anticorruption agencies will fail if they can be subjected to political direction and used as a weapon to attack critics of the government. Safeguards have to exist as well as to ensure the agency does not itself become a source for extortion and corruption.

Who should run national anticorruption agencies? Certainly not the hand-picked supporters of politicians in power. Such leaders could, at best, be relied upon not to rock the boat; at worst, they could be deployed to intimidate political opponents. Appointment procedures need to address the issue of whether the proposed mechanism sufficiently insulates the process to ensure that persons of integrity are given the leadership and that they are protected from political pressures while they are in office. Approaches widely used to provide security of tenure to high court judges could be applied here.

Checks and balances

In designing an anticorruption agency, one should consider how, in theory, the new agency would act in the worst-case scenario: that is, in response to allegations of major corruption by the nation's president. Lawmakers, after all, need to reflect on the issue of public distrust if the president is seen to be above and beyond the jurisdiction of the anticorruption authority. Establishing an agency with a special provision in its statute that highlights the power to investigate and assist the prosecution of all public officials, irrespective of rank, can strengthen a new agency and send a vital signal that builds public support from the start. A country's leaders need to accept that their successors may not share their standards and that the agency must be empowered to deal with corruption in high places.

To be sure, an anticorruption agency typically cannot prosecute presidents in office because they usually have immunity under the country's constitution. Impeachment proceedings are generally a matter for a national legislature. Accordingly, the framework of an anticorruption agency can be fashioned to enable the agency to provide reports to the leadership of the legislature, if there are reasonable grounds to believe that the president has committed an offense and if there is prima facie evidence admissible in a court of law. Similarly, the relationship between an anticorruption agency and the office of public prosecutions is critical. Agencies must be seen to have real impact leading to prosecutions and convictions. Otherwise, as has happened in several countries, they will be widely viewed as a farce. A country must have legislation that ensures the political independence not only of the anticorruption agency but also of the judiciary and the public prosecutors.

Ensuring accountability is probably the most difficult issue related to building successful anticorruption agencies. Some authorities, such as Hong Kong SAR's ICAC, have established arrangements that ensure public participation in policy formulation and oversight. By providing for such an arrangement (which could take the form of a committee chaired by the minister of justice), the anticorruption framework would encourage transparency. In Hong Kong SAR, a file that has been opened cannot be closed without the consent of the external oversight committee, which includes representatives of civil society and the private sector. This protects against corruption inside the agency.

Reaching beyond formal processes, a successful agency needs to have a charter that provides for the involvement of a wide range of people and interests in the formulation of prevention policies and their execution. In this way, various stakeholders become involved in the prevention process, and their own institutions—in both government and the private sector—can be mobilized in support of the agency's efforts. The agency's work has to be seen as meaningful, which requires that the agency be as open as possible with the press and that it publish frequent reports on its activities.

Should a new law be retroactive?

Anticorruption agencies are established to solve problems that are widely recognized. They come into being to confront, in all cases, years of corruption. Should they be focused only on the future, or should they also look to the past and investigate previous public officeholders and others who are perceived to have benefited at the public's expense? There is no certain answer, but it is evident that if a new anticorruption agency delves too deeply into past corruption it may become so overwhelmed by outstanding investigations inherited from the police that it is wholly unable to focus on the present. The legislation establishing the Hong Kong ICAC overcame the problem by stating that the commission should not, with a few exceptions; deal with matters prior to its January 1, 1977 establishment.

Conclusion

While an effective national anticorruption agency that enjoys the public's trust and that is respected by business is difficult to establish and maintain, it is all too easy to undermine. Ultimately, an anticorruption agency will be deemed successful if a nation's citizens see major public works contracts completed on time, according to plan, and with enough transparency to convince even the most skeptical observer that bribery has not been a factor. As a corruption-free, transparent project, Hong Kong's ACP has enhanced the stature of the ICAC. By contrast, Jamaica's independent contractor general's repeated reports to parliament on abuses in public procurement seem to have been consistently ignored by those on both sides of the political spectrum, undermining the credibility of Jamaica's efforts at reform.

Transparency International is convinced that greater in-depth knowledge of the successes and failures of national anticorruption agencies can be valuable. This conviction derives from the recognition that internationally coordinated efforts to curb corruption are still in their infancy and that, to ensure action and rapid results, lessons learned and best practices must be disseminated as broadly as possible.

This is not merely an academic issue. When Nigeria's President Coliseum Obasanjo was elected in the spring of 1999, he turned to many international organizations, including Transparency International, for assistance in curbing corruption, inviting detailed suggestions on how to build a new anticorruption sensitivity in the government and the institutions to support it.

He has taken the advice offered and put many ideas into practice that are now being tested. The better the advice that can be given to new leaders across the globe who are determined to confront corruption, the greater will be the chances of scoring real successes. The demand for expertise is formidable; the level of real knowledge remains at a premium. Only by pooling research and experience between public sector organizations, at the national and multilateral levels, and civil society, business, and academia can best practices be widely determined and disseminated. Building effective anticorruption agencies is one priority area where progress is being made.

Corruption is difficult to prosecute because it is shrouded in a cloud of secrecy, protected by the very same individuals we consider victims of this crime. This is precisely because most of those who partake on this practice do not see themselves as "victims" nor "accomplices," but rather as business partners closing a "profitable" deal. While they perceive this habit as producing a win-win situation, they do not realize the hidden costs that are borne by society as a whole. Creating a corruption-free government cannot be done if its citizens are also corrupt. Therefore, fighting corruption must be done by securing a partnership with the people and make them understand that everyone loses when they participate in corrupt practices. By raising their level of awareness about the ills of corruption and the extent of damage that it does to the community, the people themselves will act to eliminate this practice once and for all. Public education must focus on making people realize that everybody has a stake in fighting corruption.

Corruption and Commissions

In an effort to propagate the idea of zero tolerance for corruption, the Central Vigilance Commission (CVC) in India has begun to share with citizens a large amount of information related to corruption. The CVC website has published the names of officers from the elite administrative and revenue services against whom investigations have been ordered or penalties imposed for corruption. Newsweek magazine carried an article about this effort, calling it E-shame.

Application Context

In the Transparency International rankings for 1999, India was placed 73rd among the 99 countries rated. Corruption flourishes in India because it is perceived to be a low risk, high profit business. In service delivery, there is lack of transparency in rules and procedures, and significant delays in operations or functioning. The lack of transparency provides an opportunity for public servants to mislead citizens who have to transact business with them, and extract bribes. Certainly, the size of India's parallel economy (or black market), estimated at 40% of GDP, provides fertile ground for corruption to flourish. Equally important, the corrupt face little deterrent. There are enormous delays in the prosecution of cases in courts. What is worse, the conviction rate is hardly 6% in criminal cases.

There is a perception that corruption begins at the top, but senior bureaucrats are never investigated or punished. The main investigating agency – the Central Bureau of Investigation (CBI) – has little credibility in the eyes of the public. The Central Vigilance Commission was set up in 1964 as a Government agency. Vigilance Commissions and institutions called Lok Ayukta have also been set up and in some states. These institutions are generally headed by retired public servants or High Court judges. Their effectiveness has been mixed.

A New Approach

In 1998, based on the directive of the Supreme Court, the Government converted the Central Vigilance Commission into a statutory body through an executive order. (A bill to formalize the statutory existence of the commission was under consideration of the select committee of the Indian parliament in 2001.) The newly independent commission has taken several initiatives, particularly in recommending the use of IT by banks and other public institutions to bring in transparency. One of the initiatives was the creation of a website; and one of the first actions (January

2000) was to publish the names of senior officers who were charged with violating conduct rules. The CVC website contains the following sections/features through which the CVC communicates with the public:

1. The commission informs the public about its role, responsibility, and strategies to combat corruption. This is an effort keep the agenda of fighting corruption alive in the public mind.
2. The commissioner communicates directly with the public through messages and speeches to bolster confidence in the institution.
3. Instructions for how any citizen can lodge a complaint against corruption, without fear of disclosure or reprisal.
4. Central Vigilance Officer's List: each organization is expected to nominate a senior officer to whom an employee can take a complaint on corruption.
5. Statistical reporting of the achievements of the Commission (Annual Report).
6. Details of convictions of public servants by the courts are also presented, along with Information on officers from the All India Services against whom an enquiry has been initiated or a penalty imposed. This section also highlights the performance of various departments responsible for conducting investigations.

Although the public at large often knows who is a corrupt public servant; there has been no systematic method by which this information could be brought to the notice of either the CBI or the Income Tax department. A new feature of the CVC site will now increase the risk element for the corrupt whose ill-gotten wealth is stashed away in the form of black money, foreign accounts, benami bank accounts (wealth hidden under false names), jewelry and other valuables, benami property, etc. Members of public can now report information against a public servant about possession of black money or assets, which are believed to be disproportionate to his known sources of income. The Commission would scrutinize the information so received, and if the information is considered sufficient for carrying out detailed investigations, the CBI or the Income Tax authorities would be advised accordingly.

The Commission clearly states that it does not entertain anonymous or pseudonymous complaints. However, the identity of the complainant can be protected if he/she so desires. Section 182 of the Indian Penal Code makes it a criminal offence for a person to report about a public servant any information which he knows or believes to be false. The CBI and the Income Tax Department have schemes under which informants are rewarded for the information they provide. The informants who provide information under CVC notification also will be eligible for such rewards.

Implementation Challenges

The display of names of the senior officials of the Government of India – including IAS and IPS officers – on the CVC website in January 2000 caused a mild furor in the media. According to the CVC, the publication of these names was intended to meet a long-standing demand of the media for information about senior officials facing corruption charges and inquires. (The general perception of the public was that this kind of negative publicity appeared only against mid-level or junior officials.) Over 90 percent of those polled by the Hindustan Times welcomed the action. However, some newspapers decried the publication of the list in their editorials. Many citizens would conclude that a person is corrupt if their name appears on the website. But, in fact, only an inquiry had been ordered, which might ultimately exonerate the person.

One of the IAS Associations passed a resolution against the CVC stating that publication of a name on the site could bias the process of departmental inquiry/action. Under the law, no defamation has been caused by publicizing the names of the charged officers; yet the general perception seemed to be that the CVC website exposed a kind of a rogue's gallery. In response to these criticisms the CVC argued that all it had done was to extend to the departmental inquiries a practice that is as old as the Indian

Penal Code in criminal cases. Under criminal law, when a person is accused he is legally innocent until proven guilty; but the name of the accused enters the public domain.

Benefits and Costs

Some of those whose names have appeared on the CVC website occupied sensitive positions in government. It is a common principle in government that if a person is facing a vigilance inquiry, he should not be placed in a sensitive post. However, this practice was not being followed in India. That is one reason why corruption has flourished in the system. The CVC site brought this issue to the fore.

Another positive outcome from the site is that several people whose names appeared complained that they had never even been served with a charge sheet. Lengthy delays in the conduct of a departmental inquiry help corruption to flourish. Delay provides a cover of respectability for the guilty. Worse, perhaps, is that if departmental inquires are delayed, an innocent person may become a victim of mindless departmental procedure. His career may be ruined due to delays in getting his name cleared. The CVC now sends a monthly reminder to all departmental authorities so that the disposal of the cases may be expedited. The CVC aims to have all departmental inquires completed within six months.

The question may be raised whether in a country like India, with a low computer density; a website like the CVC's can be an effective anticorruption tool. By September 2001 only 150,000 hits had been registered on the site. Fortunately, India has a free and vibrant press. Both print media and the radio have been able to transmit the content of CVC website throughout the country. Thus, the site has had a much bigger impact than what could be expected based on India's computer density alone.

Key Lessons

Although a large volume of information is available on the CVC website, only certain specifics were picked up by the media. The publication of the names of high-placed members of government attracted significant media attention. However, when sensitive information is shared, the media must also have the ability to analyze and draw conclusions. The media will need to be educated (and educate themselves) in order to perform such a role effectively. The CVC experiment may embolden other agencies like public banks to publish the names of willful defaulters. The Governor of the Reserve Bank of India has announced that the Reserve Bank is examining this issue. Similarly, there were reports that the Department of Company Affairs was thinking of publishing the names of its defaulters.

Despite the fact that Indian society has become insensitive and cynical about corruption, the website seemed to cause some stirring of conscience. Officers whose names were published were indeed shamed. In an article, the CVC commissioner noted that some of these officers came and cried before him saying that their children were asking why their names were on the website. A poll by the Economic Times, a leading business paper of India, reported that 83 percent of respondents believed that publishing the names of charged officers on the CVC website will have a deterrent effect. Other websites run by Indian NGOs have begun to focus on corruption. For example, Tehalka.com exposed a major bribery scandal in the defense department by publishing a secretly filmed video clip on its website. Overall, Web publishing has emerged as an interesting new instrument to promote greater transparency and improved governance.

Case study author: Subhash Bhatnagar

Information used to develop the case: This case has been developed from a presentation by the Central Vigilance Commissioner in the India States Forum 2000, held in New Delhi, 23-25 November 2000, and from newspaper reports on CVC website.

STUDIES RELATED TO TEACHERS AND PARENTS ROLE

Educating the people can be done using many avenues—the formal education system, religious communities, mass media, or direct face-to-face contact. In India, schools are the targets of an NGO's initiatives to promote moral and ethical education, whose curriculum includes good citizenship and democracy. In Cambodia, a group called "Transparency Task Force" has been formed, composing educators and anti-corruption pundits, which is developing a wide-ranging, counter-corruption curriculum, which will be adopted by the Ministry of Education in its formal educational program. It is based on putting forward traditional moral and ethical values that are advanced by Cambodian folk tales and Buddhist teachings.

In Australia, on the other hand, corruption education has mainly focused on training and educating civil servants and anticorruption practitioners. In 1998, the Australian National University introduced a course on Corruption and Anti-Corruption as part of its Masters Degree in Development Administration. By using its own anti-corruption agency as an example, the ANU course trains its students on identifying where corruption starts and develop strategies to reduce or eliminate corruption entirely. The content and approach of each curriculum developed in these countries differ precisely because they are personalized to fit the culture and environment of its audience.

In Hong Kong, their anti-corruption agency has a different strategy. It educates its citizens through direct contact by setting up local offices across the region, with extended office hours and a round-the-clock hotline for complaints and reports of corruption in the community. It has also undertaken a massive publicity campaign using posters, advertisements and dramatizations of prosecuted cases in order to educate the people and at the same time, encourage them to report incidents of corruption. Coupled with harsh punitive measures and a "zero tolerance" policy from the government, it is one of the most successful models of an anticorruption agency in the world. The Philippine experience in similar undertakings has not been quite as successful, despite a long running policy against corruption at the highest level of government. The policy of using mass media as a tool to campaign for ethical behavior from civil servants has not been consistent with each change in the administration. The lack of sustainability of anti-corruption strategies is exemplified by the fact that after the Marcos regime, each succeeding president has had a different anti-corruption agency, run by political appointees, which uses the media to create hype about its investigations about cronies of the previous administration.

We might have better success in combating corruption if an anticorruption module is embedded within the curriculum of both primary and secondary schools. A strong civics background will greatly help in developing a law-abiding and responsible citizenry. Values education can also be tapped as a conduit to inculcate principles of honesty and transparency such that the opportunity to educate spreads from the school to the church, and eventually to every single household. As the typical Filipino family is closely knit, an ideal starting point for educating the youth about corruption should be at home.

Combating corruption will be truly successful if every citizen can be mobilized to act against it. In order to do so, the mass public should be educated on the evils of corruption. By explaining clearly and explicitly how ordinary citizens are personally disadvantaged by corruption in society, the public will learn that it is commonsensical to steer away from graft and corruption, and be intolerant of those who continue to practice it.

Corruption - Teacher Role

Certainly in the traditional Indian context, the teachers and the parents transmitted values. The teacher was interestingly called acharya, a word that is based on the root achar, or conduct. Thus the transmission of values was by personal example and conduct of the teacher, not by "moral science" lessons. Values were embedded in the role models of daily life. The other form of transmittal of values is via stories and exemplars. Stories that were told by grandparents and parents during childhood also have a positive role in the creation of values. Finally, the example set by parents as well as those portrayed as "successful" role models to emulate is certainly also important. In the contemporary world, mass media is a very powerful force in the creation of samskara.

In a responsible society, mass media would recognize this role rather than view its role solely as "anything goes" entertainment, blindly aping western mores or measuring its success in purely materialistic terms. But this is ultimately a matter of awakening to responsibility, not ham-handed government censorship. So, once the systematic problems are tackled, we will be at the level of the "developed" world in terms of corruption. As we mentioned earlier, the developed world is certainly no exemplar as far as morality goes. To go beyond this, one comes back to the messages of the rishis on inner transformation. This inner transformation is ultimately what can enable us to go beyond greed, avarice and a consumerism that obsessively seeks satisfaction outside oneself to move towards "santosh", a santosh that is ultimately the basis for the elimination of all corruption.

STUDIES RELATED TO SUVEYS TOWARDS CORRUPTION

Changing in India: survey

NEW DELHI, PTI

Bofors to Telgi and telecom to stock, corruption and scams have always been an inalienable part of India. But believe it or not, greasing the palms at the urban public services level is on a decline, according to a new report, indicating that corruption has moved from the mere middlemen outside the government offices level to more sophisticated areas. While, public services like regional transport offices, railways and municipal corporations are still plagued with the middlemen menace, other areas like hospitals, civil supplies, urban development, electricity and water supplies have shown a remarkable turnaround, thanks to the newfound e-governance mantra, the report released by the Centre for Media Studies says. Contrary to the popular perception that corruption is rampant, the survey which covered five major cities - Delhi, Hyderabad, Kolkata, Chennai and Mumbai - reveal that corruption in our public services has come down drastically or moved to more lucrative areas of operation, N Bhaskar Rao, CMS Chairman, says. "An interesting fact that the survey found out was corruption has come down drastically at the middlemen level. It is not high as is often believed and the reasons for this can be attributed to the large-scale computerization of services, reforms initiated by the vigilance departments and the rise in awareness among the consumers," Mr Rao says.

According to the survey, which covered eight major public utility services, corruption has shown a declining trend. Around 28 per cent of citizens who participated in the survey admitted that they have dealt through middlemen, which is a sharp decline from 48 per cent in 2000. Another 30 per cent admitted giving bribe, which was as high as 51 per cent in 2000. Interestingly, the hi-tech city of Hyderabad, where the e-seva centers are popular and widespread, the presence of middlemen and corruption has declined to 27 per cent from a whopping 63 per cent in 2000. While Kolkata and Chennai records dwindling corruption rates, 19 and 18 per cent compared to 51 and 38 per cent in 2000 respectively, Mumbai remained static and the national capital Delhi showed a spurt in corruption from 40 to 49 per cent, it says. The survey, which questioned 4500 users in these five cities, covered utility services like electricity, municipal corporation, urban development, transport, civil supplies, hospitals, water supply and railways and went into specific services like metering, billing, issue of driving license, railway ticket reservation, registration of land, and documentation. All the departments surveyed had recorded a decline in corruption levels. While municipal corporation and transport offices still topped the list corruption levels in railways and hospitals remained virtually unchanged, the survey reveals. But, despite the dip in corruption levels in these five cities, experts and officials are skeptical and have struck a cautious note as they feel corruption has disguised itself and has moved to more sophisticated areas. Corruption has shifted to more dangerous areas as softer areas are no longer available and the Telgi (stamp scam) and Dubey cases are pointers in this direction, Chief Vigilance Commissioner, P Shankar opines.

STUDIES RELATED TO CAURSE OF CORRUPTION

WHY IS INDIA POOR? CLASSIFYING THE REASONS

Before picking up individual issues on why India is poor, I'd like to classify the issues that came out of the comments. The classification is not going to be perfect, but it allows me to club the issues into manageable morsels. BTW, these are in no particular order.

- Corruption (I'd include lack of ethics in this)
- Lack of education
- Democracy (including universal adult franchise)
- Over population
- Poor Governance and Development Policies (includes resource miss- utilization, top heavy federalism, poor development, poor plan implementation, Nehruvian socialism, not enough emphasis on cities, monarchies in politics, equality "fetish", agriculture un-reformed, bureaucracy / red tape, opaque and uneven taxes)
- Lack of a strong middle class
- Culture (Lots of points get clubbed here. Acceptance / appeasement of poverty, "we hate being rich," laziness, service mentality, social and religious factors, family values, caste systems, feudalism, treating women badly, Indians are happy as they are, "monsoon complacency")
- Colonialism
- Lack of economic freedom (including lack of micro finance institutions,
- War
- Weather (Does living in the tropics make you poorer?)

If there is something I've missed out, or newer points that someone just thought of, please let me know. If you want to add a new point or change the classification, give me compelling reasons to do so.

STUDIES RELATED TO CORRUPTION RALLY

CORRUPTION - RALLY

Once again it's time for us to fight for our freedom. This time it is against the corruption. By listening to the corruption news everyday, is your blood boiling to do something for your country?

So why don't you join the largest national rally ever conducted before to generate awareness and swipe-off the corruption in India. On behalf of IndiaEyeWitness.com we want to inspire students and teachers. At the same time teachers can also collect valuable solutions to get rid of the corruption and bring up a list of best possible solutions and mail it to our honorable President, Prime Minster and the state Chief Minister. If possible send it to news media groups for public awareness. We are gathering some slogans and pamphlets, which you may use them in the rally.

STUDENTS ROLE IN THIS RALLY:

As everyone knows, "Students have the power to rewrite the history". We want you to be the initiative and be the leaders to start this rally. As a student you have the right to fight for a corruption free future. Read all the slogans provided in the website and choose the best slogan and write them on the barricades and holding boards. Print pamphlets with your suggestions to clean the corruption and distribute them during the rally. For instance, tell your parents that you don't want to grow with the money earned in a corruption deal. Ask your neighbours not to take the bribes.

TEACHERS ROLE IN THIS RALLY

Take the initiative. Motivate your students. Guide them throughout the rally process and be the leader of the rally. We request all the teachers to participate in this revolution and help them in making a peaceful rally represented by your institution. Give your ideas and collect valuable suggestions from the students in the class and create a list of best possible solutions to fight corruption. Help them in preparing the banners with slogans. Show your students a bright and corruption free future.

NRI'S ROLE IN THIS RALLY

What can an NRI do? Directly or indirectly you can participate and make this rally a great success. Since IndiaEyeWitness.Com is a no-income website, we request you to take the initiative. Sponsor an advertisement in local newspaper so that it will reach every corner of the country. Talk to your friends and families in India and let them know about this rally. Encourage and help them in whatever the form of support you can provide. Give financial support to print the pamphlets and banners for the rally. Show them what you can do to your homeland, even though you are not living there. Send an email to all your friends to spread the information as quickly as possible. Write a letter or post one of the pamphlets to your school/ College/ University where you did your education to let them know about this rally and encourage them to participate.

CONCLUSION

If there is no corruption all peoples in the world live happy. Some steps are necessary to remove corruption in the society. There is nothing in the world impossible. Principles Governing the Strategy for preventing and combating corruption:

- Adherence to the rule of law.
- Openness and accountability.
- The national will to fight corruption and to co-operate in the attainment.
- A complex approach to the war against corruption.
- Preventing corruption.
- Combating corruption.
- Educating the population.
- The National Program for preventing corruption is prepared on the basis of this strategy.
- The National Program defines priorities, allocates responsibilities and sets deadlines.

3

Statement of the Problem, Objectives, Hypotheses and Variable Studied

In the modern India, there has been a revolutionary change in the field of values due to many factors in addition to the influence of western culture industrialization, modernization, urbanization. It is necessary for us to preserve our traditional value. However, a conflict between traditional values is inevitable. It is also necessary to make efforts to present a new sense of values in a clear and complete form. One of the chief tasks of the contemporary Indian society is to bring about a synthesis of the traditional social values and modern social value.

If we give importance to social value then the corruption automatically decreased. There has been much research work in the field of corruption but no work has done on the Attitude of Scholars towards corruption. So the present investigation is intended to probe into this.

STATEMENT OF THE PROBLEM

The problem taken by the investigator for investigation is "Analytical study of the attitude of scholars towards Corruption.

This investigation is intended to the following questions specifically.

- o Is there any difference in the attitude of the male and female scholars towards corruption?
- o Is there any difference in the attitude of different religion scholars towards corruption?
- o Is there any difference in the attitude of different caste scholars towards corruption?
- o Is there any difference in the attitude of different local scholars towards corruption?

OBJECTIVES

The following are the main objectives of the present study.

- o To identify the importance of rules and regulation in the present day situation.
- o To identify the various components which influence corruption?
- o To identify in which department corruption is high.
- o To identify the relationship between corruption and education in scholars.
- o To investigate significance of corruption and with the variables like sex, locality, course of study, religion, caste, mother occupation and father occupation, mother educational qualification, father educational qualification and educational qualification of scholars.
- o To identify the solutions of the problem of corruption.

BASIC ASSUMPTION

- o Difference to exists between male and female scholars towards corruption.
- o Difference do exists between scholars who came from different local areas towards corruption.
- o Difference do exists between scholars belongs to various religions towards corruption.

- Difference do exists between scholars belongs to various casts towards corruption.
- Difference do exists between scholars in relation with whose father educational qualification.
- Difference do exists between scholars in relation with whose mother educational qualification.
- Difference do exists between scholars in relation with whose father occupation.
- Difference do exists between scholars in relation with whose mother occupation.

NEED FOR STUDY

Now we are living in the modern world. There are so many changes occurring day to day life. But all peoples are not good. Some persons are in poverty. They have no food, shelter and education. This is because of corruption in various fields. All are equal. It is necessary to give primary needs to all persons in the world. It is important to know the causes of corruption and solution for corruption. Values are important for all persons. So I taken this topic it is important to everybody.

SCOPE OF STUDY

This study is purely prepared to fine "An Analytical Study of the Attitude of Scholars towards Corruption."

This investigation is particularly done to bring out the differences if any among the scholars of sex, course of study, locality, religion, caste, mother occupation, father occupation, educational qualification of father, educational qualification of mother, educational qualification of scholars.

PURPOSE OF STUDY

The present study aims to investigate the attitudes of the scholars towards corruption. This study specifically attempts to answer the following aspects.

- Whether there is any difference in the attitudes of male and female scholars towards corruption.

- o Whether there is any difference in the attitudes of M.Phil. and Ph.D., scholars towards corruption.
- o Whether there is any difference in the attitude of scholars who came from different locality towards corruption.
- o Whether there is any difference in the attitude of scholars who belongs to different religions towards corruption.
- o Whether there is any difference in the attitude of scholars who belongs to different castes towards corruption.
- o Whether there is any difference in the attitude of scholars who belongs to different annual income categories.

METHOD OF INVESTIGATION

The study is conducted on a sample of 200 scholars (100 male and 100 female scholars)

LIMITATIONS OF THE STUDY

- o The study is limited only to the scholars of M.Phil. and Ph.D., scholars in the University.
- o The study is limited only in Tirupathi city.
- o Student of M.Tech. are not included in this study.
- o Professors, students, other staff members and administrators are not included for the purpose of this study.

VARIABLES

There are seventeen variables in this investigation. But the present investigation is chiefly concerned with sex, course of study, annual income, educational qualification of father, educational qualification mother, educational qualification of scholar, scholarship holder. occupation of mother, occupation of father, religion, caste and native place (locality).

- **Course of study**

  According to course of study M.Phil., and Ph.D., scholars were taken.
- **Sex**

  According to sex male and female scholars were taken.

- **Annual Income**

  According to annual income, Rs. up to 12,000, 12,000-25,000, 25,000-1 lokhand above one loch were included.
- **Educational qualification father**

  According to educational qualification of father, Illiterate, up to X class, Graduate and Professional were included.
- **Educational qualification of mother**

  According to educational qualification of mother, Illiterate, up to X class, Graduate and Professional were included.
- **Educational qualification of scholar**

  According educational qualification of scholar M. A./ M.Com., M.Sc., M/Phil. and Ph.D. were included.
- **Scholarship holder**

  According to scholarship holder yes or no were included.
- **Occupation of father**

  According to occupation of father, Labour, Caste occupation, Below gazetted and Gazetted were included.
- **Occupation of mother**

  According to occupation of mother, Labour/House wife and Employee were included,
- **Religion**

  According to religion Christian, Muslim and Hindu were included.
- **Caste**

  According to caste SC/ST, BC and OC were included.
- **Native place**

  According to native place, Village, Mandal Head Quarters/ Small towns and Municipal town were included.

HYPOTHESES

1. There would be no significant difference between male and female scholars towards corruption.
2. There would be no significant difference between M.Phil. and Ph.D. scholars towards corruption.

3. There would be no significant difference between scholars under the variable scholarship holder towards corruption.
4. There would be no significant difference between scholars under the variable mother occupation towards corruption.
5. There would be no significant difference among scholars under the variable educational qualification of scholar towards corruption.
6. There would be no significant difference among scholars under the variable annual income towards corruption.
7. There would be no significant difference among scholars under the variable educational qualification of father towards corruption.
8. There would be no significant difference among scholars under the variable educational qualification of mother towards corruption.
9. There would be no significant difference among scholars under the variable occupation of father towards corruption.
10. There would be no significant difference among scholars under the variable religion towards corruption.
11. There would be no significant difference among scholars under the variable caste towards corruption.
12. There would be no significant difference among scholars under the variable native place towards corruption.

CONCLUSION

The Problem taken by the investigator is very interesting. It is much and should to know about "CORRUPTION". If we destroyed the corruption in the society automatically development takes place in the country. So I request everyone tell about corruption to others.

4

Methods of Investigation

An attitude scale, specially constructed for the purpose of the study was used for collecting the data. Before describing the method used in the construction of the attitude scale, it may not be out of the place of discuss the meaning of the term 'attitude' and its nature.

MEANING OF ATTITUDE

In the dictionary of philosophy and psychology, Baldwin (1905) defined attitude as "readiness for attention or action of a definite sort".

Allport (1929) prefers to treat attitude as a mental and neutral state, a directive or dynamic influence upon the individuals' response to all objects and situations with which it is related. This definition stresses that attitude in a generalized pattern of perception or action which is the result of an integration of various experiences. From the point of view of Gestalt psychology, a change of attitude involves a definite physiology stress exerted upon a sensory field by processes originated in other parts of the nervous system (Kohler, 1929).

According to BOGARDUS (1931), ATTITUDE IS " tendency to act for or again something in the environment which becomes thereby positive or negative value". "Attitudes are literally mental postures and guides for conduct to which each new experience is referred before a response is made" (Morgan, 1935).

In the dictionary of psychology, attitude is defined as "the specific mental disposition toward an incoming (or arising) experience, where by that experience is modified or a condition of readiness for a certain type of activity" (Warren. 1934).

According to the dictionary of education (Good, 1945), an attitude is "a state of mental and emotional readiness to react to react to situations, persons, or things in a manner in harmony with these stimuli".

Guilford (1954) defined attitude as a personal disposition common to individuals, but possessed to different degrees, which impulse them to react to objects, situations, or propositions in the way that can be called favourable or unfavourable". In attitude is a dispositional readiness to respond to certain situations, persons, or objects in a constant manner which has been learned and has become ones' typical mode of response (Freeman, 1964). English and English (1958) defined attitude as "an enduring learned predisposition to behave in a consistent way towards a consistent way towards a given class of objects".

In the words of Kerechet al.962), the attitude is pro-enduring system of positive or negative evaluations, emotional feelings and process action tendencies with respect to a social object. All definitions cited above give importance to the degree of 'liking' or 'disliking' towards a psychological object and in line with the above, Thurstone (1946) defined attitude as "the degree of positive or negative affect associated with some psychological object". Though attitude and opinions are related terms they are not synonymous. Attitude is the inner feeling or belief of a person towards a psychological phenomenon, whereas opinion is what a person says out his attitude towards the phenomenon. Opinion is therefore, a verbal expression of attitude.

DIMENSIONS OF ATTITUDES

In addition to being predisposition's to respond to social objects, attitudes have been said to possess the following general characteristics.

- o Attitudes are based upon evaluative concepts regrarding motivated characteriswtics of the referent object and give rise to behaviour (Anderson and Fishbein, 1965).
- o Attitudes are constructed as verifying in quality and intensity on a continuum from positive through neutral to negative (Krech et al., 1962 and McGroth, 1964).
- o Attitudes are learned rather than being innate or a result of constitutional development and maturation (Sharif and Sharif, 1956; New Comb et al., 1959).
- o Attitudes possess the varying degree of interrelatedness to one another (Krech et al., 1962 and McGrowth, 1964).
- o Attitudes have specific social referents or specific classes there of (Kerech et al., 1962 and McGroth, 1964).
- o Attitudes are relatively stable and enduring (Newcomb et al., 1965 and Sharif, 1956).

CONSTRUCTION OF THE ATTITUDE SCALE

For the purpose of the present investigation, an attitude scale for the problem of "An Analytical Study of Scholars towards Corruption". The attitude scale was used, as the students were educated and intelligent enough to give correct responses without any chance of inhabitation or resistance on their part. The two popular and useful methods of measuring attitudes indirectly were Thurstone techniques of scale values and Likert's Method of summarized ratings. Likert's method of summed rating was used in this investigation as most of the following advantages:

- o Greater easy preparation.
- o The method is based entirely on empirical data regarding student's responses rather than subjective opinions of judges.

- o This method produces more homogenous scales and increases the probability that unitary attitude is being measures.
- o Provide more information about the student's attitude.

While constructing the attitude scale, the suggestions given by the experts in the field were considered. The summary of the suggestions were as given below:

- o Avoid that statement refers to the past rather than to the present.
- o Avoid statements that are factual or capable of being interpreted as factual.
- o Avoid statements that may be interpreted in more than one way.
- o Avoid statements that are irrelevant to the psychological object under consideration.
- o Avoid statements that are believed to cover the entire range of the effective scale of interest.
- o Select statements that are believed to cover the entire range of the effective scale of interest.
- o Keep the language of the statements simple, clear and direct.
- o Statement should be short, rarely executing twenty words.
- o Each statement should contain only one complete thought.
- o Statement containing universal such as "all", "always" "none" and "never" often those introduce ambiguity and should be avoided.
- o Words such as "only", "just", "nearly" and "others" of a singular nature should be used with care and moderation in writing statements.
- o Whenever possible statements should be in the form of simple sentences rather than in the form of compound or complex sentences.
- o Avoid the use of words that may not be understood by those who are to be given in the complete scale.
- o Avoid the use of double negative.

The following main aspects of value oriented education were taken into consideration for the preparation of the individual statements in the attitude scale.

- Purpose and functions of value oriented education
- Nature of value oriented education
- Approaches to value oriented education
- Inculcation of values
- Physical aspects of value oriented education

Bearing the above important aspects of test system in mind as a first step in the development of this questionnaire, a number if items (opinions) that are related to value oriented education were collected from the released literature and a large pool of ninety items were prepared. The pool of items, thus collected was refined by observing the criteria laid down by different authors like Likets (1932), Edwards and Kilpatrick (1954) and others.

- The statements must be clear, precise and straightforward.
- They should be short and to the point.
- They must be constructed as expressions of desired behaviour not as statements of fact.
- Double barred statements should be removed.
- They must be in a such form that the ideas can be accepted or rejected.
- Both favourable and unfavourable statements should be included.
- Statements that could be endorsed by everyone or none must be avoided.
- Positive and negative statements must be arranged randomly throughout the attitude scale so that any space error may be avoided.

Thus refined item pool was presented to the ten experienced male and female teachers who were requested to:

- Add pther statements that might be relevant to the subject
- Point out redundant statement .

- o Mark ambiguous and double barreled items, if any.
- o Give suggestions for refining the items.

Their suggestions were incorporated and seventy items were selected to be included in the preliminary form. The items were randomized each of the items was arranged on a five point scale with alternatives viz., Strongly Agree (SA), Agree (A), Doubtful (D), Disagree (DA) and Strongly Disagree (SD).

DIFFERENT METHODS OF MEASURING ATTITUDES

Attitude can be measured in several ways. Attitudes are revealed in the behaviour of an individual. So they can be measured by direct observation of overt behaviour of the individual this method, needless to point out has all the defects of observation. In addition to the difficult of experimentally creating a stimulated situation where on the behaviour can be observed.

Distinguished techniques like error technique (Hammond, 1848) sentence completion technique (Karr, 1943), story and argument completion techniques (Murray and Margpm. 1945), pictorial techniques (Smith, 1954) can also be used to assess on individuals attitudes. The basis for the use of protective techniques to measure attitude is that attitudes can be inferred by one's unconsciousness responses certain stimuli like photographs, cartoons, etc. This method's to all the disadvantages of projective technique like, difficulty in administration scoring, low inter scores, reliability etc.

The most common method of obtaining an estimate a Person's attitude is through an attitude scale. In this technique, the individual is asked to exams this opinion on several controversial statements about the psychological object under consideration. The logic behind the use of opinion to measure attitude is that they will do about it. To the extent people's actions correlated with the expressed opinion. We can naturally predict the former from the later, any single statement of opinion and any single action, however, will be extremely unreliable from the point of view of measurement. Further, though a Pearson's particular actions cannot be predicted with high degree accuracy, one's position on an attitude from expressed opinion is also subject to some limitations like faking of the response by the individual, where he tends to give socially acceptable responses there by concealing his real attitude. Nevertheless, this could be overcome in several ways like making the questionnaire anonymous, giving concealed statements etc. There are various methods of contracting attitudes scale some of them are:

- Methods of equal appearing intervals (Thurstone, 1929)
- Methods of grades dichotomists (Saffir,1937)
- Methods of summated rating (Likert, (1937)
- Scalogram analysis (Guttaman, 1944)
- Scale discrimination technique (Edwards and Kilpatrick, 1948)
- Unfolding technique (Combs, 1950)
- Method of unfolding partial rank order (Banta, 1961)
- Latent structure analysis (Lazarsfield, 1950) and
- Semantic differential (Osgood et al., 1957)

Among these, the most well known procedures are:

1. ***Thurstone's*** methods of equal appearing intervals
2. ***Likert's*** methods of summated ratings.

An overwhelming majority of scales have been developed by either of these techniques. According to Shaw and Wright (1967), this is probably a result of the greater complexity of the newer procedures. In this study, Likert's (1932) method of summated ratings is used because it is for easier than Thurston's method, but at the time yields scores very similar measure of attitude obtained by the two method was as high as 0.92 (Edwards and Henry, 1946 and Edwards, 1948).

DEVELOPMENT OF INSTRUMENT

Selection of items for Attitude Scale

To select different items for construction of attitude scale number of books and newspapers articles dealing with attitudes of corruption were reviewed and views expressed by different persons were collected in the form of statements. All the opinions thus obtained were pooled for coming-up into conclusion. All statements thus obtained were pooled and then item pool was gone through by two judges. Sixty three statements were thought most appropriate for the purpose were selected and included in the preliminary form. the statements were translated into Telugu, the regional language of Andhra Pradesh, so that the students who have passed in Telugu medium do not have any difficulty in understanding the statements.

The sixty three statements thus selected were randomized to avoid response, set on the part of respondents. Each statement was arranged on a five-point scale, Strongly Agree (SA), Agree (A), Doubtful (D), Disagree (DA) and Strongly Disagree (SDA).

TABLE 1: Weightage given to the Five alternatives responses in the scale to measure the scholars attitude towards corruption.

Type of Management	Strongly Agree	Agree	Doubtful	Disagree	Strongly Disagree
Positive	5	4	3	2	1
negative	1	2	3	4	5

In this questionnaire, the negative questions are 7,8,9,12,14,18,20,24, 25,29,31,35, 37,43,44,48,49, and 57. Remaining are positive questions. Items analysis was done, validity and reliability of the tool established as following:

Validity

The validity of a psychological tool can visualize in different connotations. The following types of validity were established.

Content Validity

This form of validity is established by evaluating the relevance of the lat items and as a whole. The construction of the present instrument items were collected from a large number of scholars and made all possible items were included. Thus, it can be reasonably assumed that the inventory has content validity.

Item Validity

The discriminative power of each the items was established by carrying out item analysis. Thus each of the items could discriminative between those who have a favourable attitude and those who did not have a favoufable attitude making the instrument valid.

Intrinsic Validity

The intrinsic validity of an instrument is defined by Guilford as the amount of true variance in the obtained scores. This is given by the square root of the reliability. The reliability scale was 0.95. Thus, the intrinsic validity of the instrument was 0.95-0.975.

Reliability

The reliability of the attitude scale was established by split half method by correlating the score obtained on the odd items with those obtained on the even items.

MAIN STUDY

Sample

The research is proximal time specific and context specific in nature. It will be very difficult for the investigator to take entire population of students studying in all existing universities. Hence, the investigator decided to take random sample to pursue his research work keeping the various variables like sex, course of study, religion, caste and native etc. Investigator conducted the questionnaire on a random sample of 200 scholars.

TABLE 2: Sample distribution according to variables

S.No.	Variables	Number
1.	Sex	
	Male	100
	Female	100
2.	Course of study	
	M.Phil.,	38
	Ph.D.,	162

3.	Scholarship holder	
	No	122
	Yes	78
4.	Mother occupation	
	Labour/House wife	191
	Employee	9
5.	Educational qualification of scholar	
	M.A/M.Com.,	59
	M.Sc.,	95
	M.Phil.,	20
	B.Ed.,	26
6.	Annual income	
	Up to 12,000 Rupess	104
	12,000-25,000	30
	25,000-1 loch	42
	Above 1 loch	24
7.	Educational qualification of father	
	Illiterate	39
	Up to X class	74
	Graduate	54
	Professional	33
8.	Educational qualification of mother	
	Illiterate	91
	Up to X class	81
	Graduate	23
	Professional	5
9.	Occupation of father	
	Labour	33
	Caste occupation	84
	Below gazited	49
	Gazited	34
10.	Religion	
	Christian	6
	Muslim	7
	Hindu	189
11	Caste	
	SC/ST	40
	BC	45
	OC	115
12.	Native place	
	Village	97
	Mandal head quarter/small town	38
	Municipal town	65

Administration

The attitude scale was administered to the sample of subject in groups of scholars in the university. Before distributing the questionnaire, the subjects were informed about the nature and significance of the work. They were informed about the nature and significance of the work. The attitude scale is self-administering. Nevertheless the instructions where read loud to the subject while they read themselves as given in the attitude scale. As there were 63 statements, the score of an individual could vary between 63 and 315 with neutral point 189.

According to Krech et al. (1962), McGrawth (1964), New Comb, Tunner and Converse (1965) attitude may be constructed as varying in quality and intensity on a continuum form positive through neutral to negative. The strength of an attitude is represented by the extremity of the position occupied by it on the continuum, becoming stronger as it goes outward from neutral position. But the neutral point of the attitude continuum possesses a problem with regard to its meaning and interpretation, to which several alternative solutions have been proposed.

First, one may consider the statement that an attitude is neutral is to self-contradictory indicationg the presence of a response predisposition on the hand and the lack of predisposition on the other. From this point of view, the neutral position on the attitude continuum represents to attitude towards the object in question (Show Wright, 1967).

The interpretation supports the idea of Krech and Crutchfield (1948) that, “Attitude always have either a positive or negative sign if they have now sign. They cannot be called attitudes at all”.

The second alternative interpretation suggested by Show and Wright (1967) is that which represents conflict, thereby reflecting an ambivalent attitude the point of balance in the positive, negative, evaluative where ambivalent is used to indicate the existence of two or more attitudes towards the same referent or several referents possessing some degree of similarity of stimulus value and being grouped as a referent class.

A mean score above the neutral point indicates that the scholars with high positive attitude towards corruption. It is needless to point out, that a mean score of say 191 just two point above the neutral point does not indicate positive attitude towards corruption, as the little difference between the mean and neutral point may be due to error variance that is bound to occur in any investigation, more so in educational and p0sychological research. Hence, the difference for significant by applying't' test.

Statistical Analysis

The data relating to the attitude score of scholars towards corruption has been summarized in a data sheet for 200 scholars according to departments, sex, religion and native. Appropriate coding was given to facilitate statistical calculations. The data is entered in excel work sheet and the analysis is done by using S.P.S.S. (Statistical Package for Social Science) software.

The mean score between two groups are compared using't' test. The mean score, S.D., mean difference and the't' value statistics have been reported in the results and significant difference between the mean scores at 0.05, 0.01 levels. The mean score among groups (more than two groups) are compared with 'F' test. The mean score, S.D., mean difference and the 'F' value have been reported in the results and significant difference among the mean scores at 0.05, 0.01 levels.

CONCLUSION

The selection of method of investigation is very important. The investigator should take care in selection of method of investigation. For my topic "An Analytical Study of Attitude of Scholars towards Corruption" I had taken Five Point Scale.

5

Analysis and Discussions

The results and discussions are analyzed in this chapter for the scores obtained.

DISTRIBUTIONS CHARACTERISTICS OF THE TTITUDINAL SCORES OF SCHOLARS TOWARDS CORRUPTION

The present investigation was conducted to study an attitude of scholars towards corruption.

The total attitudinal score of the each individual is calculated and presented in the form of frequency distribution.

TABLE 3: Frequency distribution of attitudinal score of total scholars towards corruption

S.No.	CI	MP	F	CF
1	210-219	214.5	4	4
2	220-229	224.5	6	10
3	230-239	234.5	10	20
4	240-249	244.5	23	43
5	250-259	254.5	37	80
6	260-269	264.5	28	108
7	270-279	274.5	44	152
8	280-289	284.5	31	183
9	290-299	294.5	14	197
10	300-309	304.5	3	200

Mean = 264.92
Median = 267.00
Mode = 272.00
SD = 19.49
Skew ness = -0.353
Kurtosis = .298
Q1 = 252.25
Q3 = 279.00
Q.D = 13.375

From the table it is clear that the mean scores of scholars towards corruption for total sample 200 is 264.92. Since Mean, Median, Mode are not same, the curve not be a normal, the kurtosis obtained is .298 is slightly greater than 0.263. The peak of the curve is platy. In this distribution mean is less than median. So the skew ness is negative. The peak is shifted towards left.

TABLE 4: Frequency distribution of attitudinal scores of male scholars towards corruption.

S.No.	CI	MP	F	CF
1	210-219	214.5	1	1
2	220-229	224.5	4	5
3	230-239	234.5	3	8
4	240-249	244.5	11	19
5	250-259	254.5	24	43
6	260-269	264.5	19	62
7	270-279	274.5	17	89
8	280-289	284.5	13	92
9	290-299	294.5	6	98
10	300-309	304.5	2	100

Mean = 264.00
Median = 264.00
Mode = 255.00
SD = 18.481
Skew ness = 0.336
Kurtosis = 0.054
Q1 = 253
Q3 = 278
Q.D = 12.5

From the table it is clear that the mean scores of male scholars towards corruption for total sample 100 is 264.00. Since Mean, Median, Mode are not same, the curve not be a normal, the kurtosis obtained is .336 is greater than 0.263. The peak of the curve is platy. In this distribution mean is equal to median and greater than mode. So the skew ness is positive. The peak is shifted towards right.

TABLE 5: Frequency distribution of attitudinal scores of female scholars towards corruption.

S.No.	CI	MP	F	CF
1	210-219	214.5	3	3
2	220-229	224.5	2	5
3	230-239	234.5	7	12
4	240-249	244.5	12	24
5	250-259	254.5	13	37
6	260-269	264.5	9	46
7	270-279	274.5	27	73
8	280-289	284.5	18	91
9	290-299	294.5	8	99
10	300-309	304.5	1	100

Mean = 265.77
Median = 272.00
Mode = 272.00
SD = 20.507
Skew ness = -0.189
Kurtosis = 0.60
Q1 = 251
Q3 = 281
Q.D = 15

From the table it is clear that the mean scores of female scholars towards corruption for total sample 100 is 265.77. Since Mean, Median, Mode are not same, the curve not be a normal, the kurtosis obtained is 0.189 is less than 0.263. The peak of the curve is lepto. In this distribution mean is less than median and mode. So the skew ness is negative. The peak is shifted towards left.

CONSOLIDATED MEANS, SDs,'t' AND 'F' VALUES OF VARIOUS VARIABLES:

TABLE 6: Means and SDs of different variables and subgroups of scholars towards corruption in respective 't' and 'F' values.

Variables	Categories	N	Mean	SD	't' value
Sex	Male	100	264.07	18.481	0.6158
	Female	100	265.77	20.507	@
Course of	M.Phil.,	38	263.76	18.749	0.419
study	Ph.D.,	162	265.19	19.705	@
Scholarship	No	122	265.20	19.356	0.256
holder	Yes	78	264.47	19.814	@
Mother	Labour/HW	191	264.92	19.454	0.004
occupation	Employee	9	264.89	21.444	@
Educational	M.A./M.Com	59	263.36	19.145	'F' value
qualification	M.Sc.	95	266.61	18.439	
	M.Phil.	20	259.45	23.712	0.731
	B.Ed.	26	266.50	20.598	@
Annual	Up to 12,000	104	264.63	18.825	
income	12,00-25,000	30	264.10	22.310	
	25,000-1 loch	42	264.12	19.848	1.223
	1 loch above	24	268.62	18.782	@
Educational	Illiterate	39	262.26	19.597	
qualification	Up to X class	74	264.46	18.436	
Of father	Graduate	54	265.52	20.998	0.547
	Professional	33	268.12	19.496	@
Educational	Illiterate	91	264.74	20.017	
qualification	Up to X class	81	265.32	19.151	
of mother	Graduate	23	262.43	20.385	0.390
	Professional	5	273.20	11.670	@
Occupation	Labour	33	260.06	20.538	
of father	Caste occupa	84	265.99	17.786	
	Below Gaze	49	264.59	20.866	1.487
	Gazetted	34	267.47	20.476	@
	Christian	6	265.00	22.307	
Religion	Muslim	7	267.29	25.519	0.29
	Hindu	189	264.88	19.282	@
	SC/ST	40	259.57	21.945	
Caste	BC	45	266.93	17.591	0.454
	OC	115	265.99	19.134	@
	Village	97	265.19	18.205	
Native place	MHQ/ST	38	263.87	19.154	0.546
	Municipal T	65	265.14	21.703	@

IMPACT OF VARIOUS VARIABLES ON THE ATTITUDE TOWARDS CORRUPTION.

Hypothesis-1

There would be no significant difference between male and female scholars towards corruption.

The above hypothesis is tested by employing 't' test and the results are shown in the table.

Table 7: Mean and SDs of attitudinal scores of scholars towards corruption under the variable sex.

Sex	N	Mean	SD	't' value
Male	100	264.04	18.481	0.6158
Female	100	265.77	20.507	@

@ 't' not significant at 0.05 level

It is clear from the table that the calculated 't' value 0.6158 is less than the table value 197 for 198 df at 0.05 level. It is not significant at 0.05 level. Hence, the null hypothesis is accepted. It is concluded that there is no significant difference between male and female scholars towards corruption.

Hypothesis-2

There would be no significant difference between M.Phil., and Ph.D., scholars towards corruption.

The above hypothesis is tested by employing't' test and the results are shown in the table.

Table 8: Mean and SDs of attitudinal scores of scholars towards corruption under the variable course of study.

Course of stu	N	Mean	SD	't' value
M.Phil.,	38	263.76	18.749	0.419
Ph.D.,	162	265.19	19.705	@

@ 't' not significant at 0.05 level

It is clear from the table that the calculated 't' value 0.419 is less than the table value 197 for 198 df at 0.05 level. It is not significant at 0.05 level. Hence, the null hypothesis is accepted. It is concluded that there is no significant difference between scholars towards corruption under the variable course of study.

Hypothesis-3

There would be no significant difference between scholars towards corruption under the variable scholarship holder.

The above hypothesis is tested by employing't' test and the results are shown in the table.

Table 9: Mean and SDs of attitudinal scores of scholars towards corruption under the variable scholarship holder.

SSH	N	Mean	SD	't' value
No	122	265.20	19.356	0.256
Yes	78	264.47	19.814	@

@ 't' not significant at 0.05 level

It is clear from the table that the calculated't' value 0.256 is less than the table value 197 for 198 df at 0.05 level. It is not significant at 0.05 level. Hence, the null hypothesis is accepted. It is concluded that there is no significant difference between scholars towards corruption under the variable scholarship holder.

Hypothesis-4

There would be no significant difference between scholars towards corruption under the variable mother occupation.

The above hypothesis is tested by employing 't' test and the results are shown in the table.

Table 10: Mean and SDs of attitudinal scores of scholars towards corruption under the variable mother occupation.

Mother Occu	**N**	**Mean**	**SD**	**'t' value**
Labour/HW	191	264.92	19.454	0.004
Employee	9	264.89	21.444	@

@ 't' not significant at 0.05 level

It is clear from the table that the calculated 't' value 0.004 is less than the table value 197 for 198 df at 0.05 level. It is not significant at 0.05 level. Hence, the null hypothesis is accepted. It is concluded that there is no significant difference between scholars towards corruption under the mother occupation.

Hypothesis-5

There would be no significant difference among the scholars towards corruption under the variable educational qualification.

The above hypothesis is tested by employing 'F' test and the results are shown in the table.

Table 11: Summary of Analysis of variance (ANOVA) for the attitudinal scores of scholars towards corruption under the variable educational qualification of scholars.

Score	SS	df	MS	'F' value
Between groups	99237.121	3	33079.040	
Within groups	8871832	196	45264.447	0.731
Total	8971069	199		@

@ 'F' not significant at 0.05 level.

It is clear from the table that the calculated 'F' value 0.731 is less than the table value2.65 for 3 and 196 df at 0.05 level. It is not significant at 0.05 level. Hence, the null hypothesis is accepted. It is concluded that there is no significant difference among scholars towards corruption under the variable educational qualification.

Hypothesis-6

There would be no significant difference among the scholars towards corruption under the variable annual income.

The above hypothesis is tested by employing 'F' test and the results are shown in the table.

Table 12: Summary of Analysis of variance (ANOVA) for the attitudinal scores of scholars towards corruption under the variable annual income.

Score	SS	df	MS	'F' value
Between groups	1648656	3	54955.205	
Within groups	8806203	196	44929.608	1.223
Total	8971069	199		@

@ 'F' not significant at 0.05 level.

It is clear from the table that the calculated 'F' value 1.223 is less than the table value2.65 for 3 and 196 df at 0.05 level. It is not significant at 0.05 level. Hence, the null hypothesis is accepted. It is concluded that there is no significant difference among scholars towards corruption under the variable annual income.

Hypothesis-7

There would be no significant difference among the scholars towards corruption under the variable educational qualification of father.

The above hypothesis is tested by employing 'F' test and the results are shown in the table.

Table 13: Summary of Analysis of variance (ANOVA) for the attitudinal scores of scholars towards corruption under the variable educational qualification of father.

Score	SS	df	MS	'F' value
Between groups	74508287	3	24836.096	
Within groups	8896560	196	45390.614	0.547
Total	8971069	199		@

@ 'F' not significant at 0.05 level.

It is clear from the table that the calculated 'F' value 0.547 is less than the table value2.65 for 3 and 196 df at 0.05 level. It is not significant at 0.05 level. Hence, the null hypothesis is accepted. It is concluded that there is no significant difference among scholars towards corruption under the variable educational qualification of father.

Hypothesis-8

There would be no significant difference among the scholars towards corruption under the variable educational qualification of mother.

The above hypothesis is tested by employing 'F' test and the results are shown in the table.

Table 14: Summary of Analysis of variance (ANOVA) for the attitudinal scores of scholars towards corruption under the variable educational qualification of mother.

Score	SS	df	MS	'F' value
Between groups	53299.624	3	17766.541	
Within groups	8917769	196	45498.822	0.390
Total	8971069	199		@

@ 'F' not significant at 0.05 level.

It is clear from the table that the calculated 'F' value 0.390 is less than the table value2.65 for 3 and 196 df at 0.05 level. It is not significant at 0.05 level. Hence, the null hypothesis is accepted. It is concluded that there is no significant difference among scholars towards corruption under the variable educational qualification of mother.

Hypothesis-9

There would be no significant difference among the scholars towards corruption under the variable occupation of father.

The above hypothesis is tested by employing 'F' test and the results are shown in the table.

Table 15: Summary of Analysis of variance (ANOVA) for the attitudinal scores of scholars towards corruption under the variable occupation of father.

Score	SS	df	MS	'F' value
Between groups	199672.5	3	66557.485	
Within groups	8771396	196	44752.022	1.487
Total	8971069	199		@

@ 'F' not significant at 0.05 level.

It is clear from the table that the calculated 'F' value 1.487 is less than the table value2.65 for 3 and 196 df at 0.05 level. It is not significant at 0.05 level. Hence, the null hypothesis is accepted. It is concluded that there is no significant difference among scholars towards corruption under the variable occupation of father.

Hypothesis-10

There would be no significant difference among the scholars towards corruption under the variable religion.

The above hypothesis is tested by employing 'F' test and the results are shown in the table.

Table 15: Summary of Analysis of variance (ANOVA) for the attitudinal scores of scholars towards corruption under the variable religion.

Score	SS	df	MS	'F' value
Between groups	2622.372	2	1311.186	
Within groups	8968446	197	45525.108	0.029
Total	8971069	198		@

@ 'F' not significant at 0.05 level.

It is clear from the table that the calculated 'F' value 0.029 is less than the table value2.65 for 2 and 197 df at 0.05 level. It is not significant at 0.05 level. Hence, the null hypothesis is accepted. It is concluded that there is no significant difference among scholars towards corruption under the variable religion.

Hypothesis-11

There would be no significant difference among the scholars towards corruption under the variable caste.

The above hypothesis is tested by employing 'F' test and the results are shown in the table.

Table 16: Summary of Analysis of variance (ANOVA) for the attitudinal scores of scholars towards corruption under the variable caste.

Score	SS	df	MS	'F' value
Between groups	41145.849	2	20572.925	
Within groups	8929923	197	45329.558	0.454
Total	8971069	198		@

@ 'F' not significant at 0.05 level.

It is clear from the table that the calculated 'F' value 0.454 is less than the table value2.65 for 2 and 197 df at 0.05 level. It is not significant at 0.05 level. Hence, the null hypothesis is accepted. It is concluded that there is no significant difference among scholars towards corruption under the variable caste.

Hypothesis-12

There would be no significant difference among the scholars towards corruption under the variable native place.

The above hypothesis is tested by employing 'F' test and the results are shown in the table.

Table 17: Summary of Analysis of variance (ANOVA) for the attitudinal scores of scholars towards corruption under the variable native place.

Score	SS	df	MS	'F' value
Between groups	49428.871	2	24714.436	
Within groups	8921640	197	45287.512	0.546
Total	8971069	198		@

@ 'F' not significant at 0.05 level.

It is clear from the table that the calculated 'F' value 0.029 is less than the table value2.65 for 2 and 197 df at 0.05 level. It is not significant at 0.05 level. Hence, the null hypothesis is accepted. It is concluded that there is no significant difference among scholars towards corruption under the variable native place.

6

Summary, Conclusions and Suggestions

SUMMARY

A shortage of basic decent human life in India has forced a common person to be corrupt. It is impossible for a common man to own a roof, provide good education to his children and hope for a peaceful retirement in India using normal and honest means. One has to bribe someone to get a good education, to get a deserving job and to avail services which one is entitled as being a citizen of India. A two percent growth rate in the GDP for two decades and explosive population growth in the last fifty years has brought corruption to every sphere of life in India. With such a huge population and massive government control, everything seems to be in short supply.

In India, government controls education, means of daily transportation, heavy industry like steel and automobile production, oil and gas production and distribution, public works departments, irrigation, banking, power generation and distribution, water purification and distribution, distribution of basic food commodities to individuals living below the poverty line, defense, hospitals, police, judiciary and dozens of other areas affecting its citizens' day-to-day life. Declining real wages has forced the government employees to use their position to extort money from other civilians to fulfill obligations towards their families. Criminalization of politics and poorly qualified politicians has further enabled sometimes forced these employees to misuse their authority. It is common to secure favors in various state and central government by bribing elected politicians. Ministers openly ask government employee to bring huge sums to return favors. A financially lucrative posting and award of government contracts are the big routes to funnel tax payer's money back to ruling party and politician's personal accounts. Domino effect of such bribes can be seen to the lowest level of the society. Government contracts run over budget. Hence the deficits in the government budgets keep on growing. On the other side, contractors performing these jobs squeeze the common labor to make their profits. Poor roads, inadequate drinking water supply in villages and acute housing shortage in various cities are few of a long list resulting from such government controlled environment. Farmers have to bribe government controlled bank officials to get an approval for a loan to buy tractors or other machinery. One has to bribe another set of government employees to get permits and basic supplies needed for developing any personnel and commercial property. Poor infrastructure and underdevelopment of villages is a direct result of such government control. Government's total failure in power generation and distribution has substantially added to such underdevelopment.

Corruption has also seeped in the poorly paid police and the judiciary system. Traffic laws in India seem to be the worst in the world. One can bribe a government official to get a driver's license without even taking a driving test. A small bribe on the spot to a traffic policeman can save a traffic ticket or a court trip. Most of the government controlled schools and colleges run short of teachers and other staff. Most of the teachers at the school level almost force students to take private lessons from them by avoiding any teaching in the schools. Colleges are run by poorly qualified or without any teachers at all. Poor quality of education provided in the government schools has forced individuals to pursue private schools out of their financial reach. This further forces individuals in power to be more corrupt. This in a long run has divided our society in distinct educated and totally illiterate groups.

Seniority or caste based promotions in government controlled jobs force most individuals to take bribes to fulfill their responsibilities otherwise impossible to cater on ever declining wages. With closed economy, quality products are in limited supply. Normal individuals have to bribe someone to buy quality products used in day-to-day life. Basically, such massive government involvement in an ordinary citizen's life has helped corruption to grow leaps and bound. With loose campaign financing rules, millions of rupees are funneled in various political parties' election fund from the major industrial houses. This results in higher prices of the goods used by the general public. Subsidies in the name of poor, which never reach to the one intended, facilitate corruption in more government employees. Government's funding of inefficient steel plants, oil refineries, fertilizer and chemical plants and other massive money losing public sector is a direct result of poorly managed and highly corrupt administration.

Corruption in India can not be eradicated by questioning ethical standards of its population. Removal of corruption can only be achieved by right macro-economic policies and by reducing government control. Honest political leadership is a must as a first step. Opening the economy for the investors around the world can provide the needed capital. Fresh ideas and entrepreneurial spirit has to replace the beauracratic government control for a wealthier society. Supply of basic commodities has to be higher than the demand for general population to not bribe any government officials. Only skilled entrepreneurs hired by public shareholders can bring the money loosing monster public sector to profitability. An efficient tax collection mechanism supported by computerized revenue reporting systems of individual businesses would be a step in the right direction. Qualified political leadership is required to understand and implement such policies.

Most importantly, political will of these leaders will be required to take such actions.

In conclusion, corruption in India exists because of the unfulfillment of the basic needs of the general population. To eradicate corruption, India has to implement right macro-economic policies rather than questioning the ethical standards of its population.

Towards Change

How then do we create change in the system so that it is more responsive to the people, more fulfilling to the employees and more effective for the nation? The following steps should be considered, in order of importance:

1. Reducing the size of the government and privatizing non-essential functions.
2. De-centralizing government functions away from large hierarchical bureaucracies and creating greater local accountability.
3. Simplifying laws, rules and procedures, taking into account the actual needs and practices of the people and creating a greater focus on customer service in public institutions.
4. Simplifying taxation, reducing duties on property taxes and property transfers and creating greater transparency and "buy-in" for the use of tax-proceeds by devolving more taxation and spending to local administration from the center and states
5. Tackling campaign finance reform – realizing that elections today involve large expenditures and creating rules for legal campaign contributions that take this into account while reducing the influence of criminal/black money clear performance-based reward system within the government to create greater incentive for honesty and performance.
6. More effective enforcement and prosecution of the remaining corrupt personnel to increase the cost for the corrupt.

The first fact to realize is that the answer is not more rules and larger bureaucracies, but a more transparent, accountable and responsive system. One option there is simply greater privatization where market demand and competition will drive accountability.

The telephone example is again a good one. If we are fundamentally corrupt, why is it that we do not have to pay a bribe in India to get a mobile phone? How would the situation have been different if mobile phones were to be a government monopoly instead? The answer is simple – in the case of competitive private enterprise, it is in the interests of the private operator to provide greater customer service – it is only in a monopoly where these interests are divergent. Some of these aligning of interests can also happen in semi-private models. In a recent journey on a local bus in Delhi, I was pleased to find courteous service and the conductor making sure that I got a ticket. Later I was told that the driver and conductor now get a percentage of the proceeds and both the quality of service and the revenue that is collected by the government has gone up as a result.

Secondly, a restructuring of government function needs to happen so that there is far greater local accountability. Let us take the example of education. Currently, appointments and administration of teachers for schools are centralized at the level of the entire state. This means that accountability flows into the state level bureaucracy that is itself only accountable to the ministers. Since the ministers are elected, it turns out that the loop of accountability to the consumers is closed only at the highest level. This is inefficient and frustrating at all levels. The teachers find that they are subject to arbitrary transfers by bureaucrats, the end consumers are not in the loop at all of teacher accountability or performance, the ministers find themselves deluged with personal requests for low-level appointments and the bureaucrats find themselves at the mercy of politicians. I recently met one of the senior-most bureaucrats in the state of Rajasthan with a reputation for honesty. A visit to his house showed that he had a very simple lifestyle. However, he was despondent about his lack of ability to make change. “Everything in this system is delegated upwards,” he said. “Even the transfer of a chapprassi will come as an order from the minister.” Clearly, the system serves no one well.

Taxation is another area of reform. Land and property transactions as well as local retail sales remain areas of high black money generation. There was a time when capital gains on sales of property were as high as 66%. No one in their right mind, after holding property for twenty years, would pay 66% of it in tax to the government – especially when the government appeared as a black hole of antagonistic incompetence, serving very little useful purpose. While this has been reduced, property transfers still remain expensive transaction with high stamp duties. Devolving more taxes down to the local community level, where the benefits of the government expenditures are both more visible and more accountable, will also help in this regard.

It is also worth noting that greater prosecution of corrupt officials has been placed last in this list even though it often receives the greatest emphasis from anti-corruption crusaders. This is because enforcement, while necessary, will remain ineffective in tackling the magnitude of the problem in the absence of systematic reform. At the present time, community activism can yield better long-term results when directed towards crafting a more responsive system than simply pursuing a few high-profile enforcement cases.

Similarly, continuing to harp on corruption as simply a moral problem without addressing first the issues of systemic reform exacerbates the problem of corruption rather than helping it. This is because if the problem is that we are corrupt, it becomes very difficult to change anything, since it is obviously very difficult to change who we are as people. It is no surprise that in the light of this belief; very few people in India believe that we can fix the problem of corruption. Realizing that much of it is a problem of the system can be an empowering and actionable idea, even while the road may be long. It is worth remembering that, even with all the problems in the Indian system, it still survives and functions because there remain a remarkable number of honest people trying to do their jobs, despite all the difficulties and disincentives. It is this honesty that we must build on and nourish as we create a blueprint for deep, systematic changes.

Views on Governance

I think definitely there is a need for improved Governance. Now a days Governance has become a big buzzword ever since in the corporations started going under all kind of misuse coming in so the word corporate Governance has become very fashionable. Also everybody is aware of the failure of the Governance of Government, as there is a lot of corruption, objectives are not being met, there are slippages and therefore the results don't trickle down. They might have excellent policy but when it comes to implementation it is just not reaching the people for whom it is meant. So everybody becomes very conscious of the need of better Governance by Government and then I think logically it is coming down to the non-profit sector.

Till now everybody was content that it is going at enormous pace. There was need that government began realizing the need of Ngos to take up some services, which they are not successfully admitting. All of a sudden there was an increased inflow of funds and for that reason people became conscious of funds being properly utilized. I think today there is far more awareness of the need to give on the part of the better off than there was so many years ago. The question of transparency and accountability started because of inflow of funds and therefore the question of Governance. It is about utilization of funds in not just pure accounting sense but it is also in the sense of achieving objectives.

It is inevitable in the sense that with Globalization coming, we are talking about increased efficiency particularly among corporate sector. Even Indian corporate were pretty content in a protective situation to produce what they want as they knew that there will be always a demand, so with the globalization coming in, competition came in and the also the realization of increasing the efficiency. I think the same thing is happening in the Ngos sector.

Till now it was almost taken for granted that the non-profits were synonymous to dedication and commitment and cost flexibility was considered a good norm to achieve the end results. Sometimes the pendulum swung a little too far and lot of inefficiencies of all kind crept in. People tend to take things easy.

There were organizations that got lots of money and some did not so there was this question of having to improve the performance of the organization in order to attract founders. You will only be able to get money only if you are seen by your donors. Today, with more need of funding, NGOs have to raise the money from the public also and public will support you only if they think that you are good and honest. Governance means are you giving satisfaction to all your stakeholders and not just the donors. Are you meeting all the commitments to your primary constituency, whoever it is? Are you complying with all the laws? Today, one has to look governance in all these lines.

Most of the times the members of governing body are too busy to get deeply involved in the organization. I think that also has to change even though they are voluntary board. They should take more responsibility if they want to be seen as Governing an organization because ultimately the authority rest in the governing body. From there it goes down to all other hierarchies in the organization. So I think definitely there is need and it will come and a lot of corporate practices will start getting incorporated to the extent they are relevant because of the same Globalization. There is a lot of cross-fertilization both internationally and between sectors and all that is going to reflect.

Indian culture is beautiful. All persons in the world like Indian culture. Unity in diversity is the special thing of India. India is a rich country. But Indians are poor. There are many causes for this one. Un-education, lack of communication and old traditions (not all only something).

There are so many books about honesty, truth, peace and non-violence. But is important to implement them. Other wise there is no use.

If our behaviour is good then only we will see good behaviour in others. My opinion all problems have one solution that is education.

Swamy Vivekananda, Mahatma Gandhi, Nehru, Indira Gandhi, Rajiv Gandhi are dynamic leaders gave a valuable speech. Those are very important for us.

PROBLEM

From the past, value oriented education is existing in India. It takes diversified changes in the ancient, medieval and modern periods. When India freed from the Britishers in 1947, again various changes occurred in educational system. We studied about many honest persons in Purina and Vedas. At that time each and every person honest. By increasing population and technology the selfishness of the person increases. It gives so many problems, some research work done on corruption. I liked to know the attitude of scholars towards corruption. So my problem is "The Analytical Study of Attitude of Scholars towards Corruption".

SAMPLE

The sample for the investigation was selected by a multistage stratified random sampling procedure, it consists of 200 scholars. All the scholars belonging to the various departments in the universities like Sri Venkateswara University, Padmavathi Mahila Viswa Vidyalayam and Samskrutha Vidya Peet.

Tools and techniques used

An attitude scale specially designed and administered for the study of the attitude of scholars towards corruption was used to collect the data for the investigation. Present study aims at An Analytical Study of Corruption on different areas. To measure the attitude of scholars investigator used the five point scale comprises of 63 items. Against each of them five alternatives were given. They are SA, A, D, DA, SDA. In the scale among 63 items 19 are negative and all the remainings are positive.

CONCLUSIONS

The conclusions drawn from hypothesis is tested were as follows.

Hypothesis-1

An analysis of the mean attitudinal scores of male and female scholars showed that there was no significant difference between tow groups with regard to this attitude towards corruption. Both have positive attitude towards corruption but there was no significant difference in this attitude.

Thus, the hypothesis-1 viz., "There was no significant difference between male and female scholars towards corruption" was accepted.

Hypothesis-2

An analysis of the mean attitudinal scores of scholars under the variable course of study showed that there was no significant difference between tow groups with regard to this attitude towards corruption. Both have positive attitude towards corruption but there was no significant difference in this attitude.

Thus, the hypothesis-2 viz., "There was no significant difference between M .Phil. And Ph. D. scholars towards corruption" was accepted.

Hypothesis-3

An analysis of the mean attitudinal scores of scholars under the variable scholarship holder showed that there was no significant difference between two groups with regard to this attitude towards corruption. Both have positive attitude towards corruption but there was no significant difference in this attitude.

Thus, the hypothesis-3 viz., "There was no significant difference between scholars under the variable scholarship holder towards corruption" was accepted.

Hypothesis-4

An analysis of the mean attitudinal scores of scholars under the variable mother occupation showed that there was no significant difference between two groups with regard to this attitude towards corruption. Both have positive attitude towards corruption but there was no significant difference in this attitude.

Thus, the hypothesis-4 viz., "There was no significant different between scholars under the variable mother occupation towards corruption" was accepted.

Hypothesis-5

An analysis of the mean attitudinal scores of scholars under the variable educational qualification showed that there was no significant difference among four groups with regard to this attitude towards corruption. Four have positive attitude towards corruption.

Thus, the hypothesis-5 viz., "There was no significant difference among scholars under the variable educational qualification towards corruption" was accepted.

Hypothesis-6

An analysis of the mean attitudinal scores of scholars under the variable annual income showed that there was no significant difference among four groups with regard to this attitude towards corruption. Four have positive attitude towards corruption.

Thus, the hypothesis-6 viz., "There was no significant difference among scholars under the variable annual income towards corruption" was accepted.

Hypothesis-7

An analysis of the mean attitudinal scores of scholars under the variable father educational qualification showed that there was no significant difference among four groups with regard to this attitude towards corruption. Four have positive attitude towards corruption.

Thus, hypothesis-7 viz., "There was no significant difference among scholars under the variable father educational qualification towards corruption" was accepted.

Hypothesis-8

An analysis of the mean attitudinal scores of scholars under the variable mother educational qualification showed that there was no significant difference among four groups with regard to this attitude towards corruption. Four have positive attitude towards corruption.

Thus, hypothesis-8 viz., "There was no significant difference among scholars under the variable mother educational qualification towards corruption" was accepted.

Hypothesis-9

An analysis of the mean attitudinal scores of scholars under the variable father occupation showed that there was no significant difference among four groups with regard to this attitude towards corruption. Four have positive attitude towards corruption.

Thus, the hypothesis-9 viz., "There was no significant difference among scholars under the variable father occupation towards corruption" was accepted.

Hypothesis-10

An analysis of the mean attitudinal scores of scholars under the variable religion showed that there was no significant difference among four groups with regard to this attitude towards corruption. Three have positive attitude towards corruption. Thus, the hypothesis-10 viz., "There was no significant difference among scholars under the variable religion towards corruption" was accepted.

Hypothesis-11

An analysis of the mean attitudinal scores of scholars under the variable caste showed that there was no significant difference among four groups with regard to this attitude towards corruption. Three have positive attitude towards corruption. Thus, the hypothesis-11 viz., "There was no significant difference among scholars under the variable caste towards corruption" was accepted.

Hypothesis-12

An analysis of the mean attitudinal scores of scholars under the variable native place showed that there was no significant difference among four groups with regard to this attitude towards corruption. Four have positive attitude towards corruption. Thus, the hypothesis-12 viz., "There was no significant difference among scholars under the variable native place towards corruption" was accepted.

EDUCATIONAL IMPLICATIONS

CURRICULAR ACTIVITIES

In this investigation; it was found that the study of attitudes of scholars towards Corruption. Due to liberalization, industrialization and globalization rapid changes are occurring in almost all social sciences. The value possessed and their attitudes according to the changes should be known up to date vast changes are occurring in the education. So called philosophical foundations of India are declining day to day with the country in a state of social turbulence, the goals and functions of formal education need to be reassessed and updated. Through education we can change the world.

The Educational implication of corruption through curriculum can be described as follows:

- By giving a place for corruption in the curriculum.
- Corruption can be explained through Stories and illustrations.
- Corruption Education has mainly focused on training and educating civil servants and anti corruption practitioners.

- o By introducing a course on corruption and anti-corruption as part of its Master Degree in Developmental Administration.
- o Giving course training to students on identifying where corruption starts and develop strategies to reduce or eliminate corruption entirely.
- o By educating citizen through direct contact by setting up local offices across the religion.
- o Educate people through posters, advertisements and dramatizations; those are all a part in the curriculum.
- o By telling moral and ethical stories in the class room.
- o Role play of a good story in the lesson.

Co-curricular activities:

- o Arranging excursions, field trips and service camps and making the scholars/students to participate actively in them.
- o Organizing service agencies like JRC, Scouting, NSS, Clubs, Association, etc.
- o Arranging debates, discussions, essay writing competitions etc., on topics like National Integration, Literacy Mission.
- o Celebration birthdays of national leaders, important persons and events.
- o Arranging inter-collegiate and intra-university sports, athletics, games, etc.
- o Dramatization and role play.
- o Making the students responsible in various school managements and college activities-student/scholar participation.
- o Organization of science clubs, literary associations, music centers, recreational centers, adult education programs etc.
- o Organization morning prayers, celebrating certain socio-cultural festivals, anniversaries, school day, teachers' day, parent-teacher association meeting etc.

- Encouraging values in the students by giving the talented and devoted persons awards, gifts, titles, rolling shields etc.
- Telling about good stories about values and corruption.
- Conducting different types of competitions regarding to corruption.
- Giving suggestion to read good books regarding to corruption.

LIMITATIONS

- In this investigation, an attempt was made to study the attitude of scholars towards corruption as viewed by the scholars themselves.
- The investigation need not pointed out scholar's attitude with department wise towards corruption.
- This investigation is done only 200 samples of scholars in Tirupathi universities only. An analytical study may be done on large sample scholars attitude towards corruption.
- The investigation is done only scholars of M.Phil., and Ph.D.
- This investigation is done only in Chittoor district.

SUGGESTIONS FOR FURTHER RESEARCH

Scholars' attitude towards corruption further research may be done in the following areas.

- The Attitude of High School children may be studied towards corruption.
- The Attitude of Junior College Students may be studied towards corruption.
- The Attitude of Degree College Students may be studied towards corruption.
- The Attitude of M.Sc., M.Com. and M.A. Students may be studied towards corruption.
- The Attitude of M.C.A. and M.B.A. Students may be studied towards corruption.

- o The Attitude of Engineering College Students may be studied towards corruption.
- o The investigation may be done in the other district and state.
- o The Attitude of Medical Students may be studied towards corruption.
- o The investigation can be carried out on a large sample belonged to different states in our country.
- o The Attitude in this study confirmed to only scholars but may be extended to various fields like teachers, PMT, TGT, PGTs towards corruption.

INVESTIGATOR THOUGHT

My opinion Education is a solution for any type of problem in the world. We can solve all type of problems through education.

Corruption is difficult to prosecute because it is shrouded in a cloud of secrecy, protected by the very same individuals we consider victims of this crime. This is precisely because most of those who partake on this practice do not see themselves as "victims" nor "accomplices," but rather as business partners closing a "profitable" deal. While they perceive this habit as producing a win-win situation, they do not realize the hidden costs that are borne by society as a whole.

Creating a corruption-free government cannot be done if its citizens are also corrupt. Therefore, fighting corruption must be done by securing a partnership with the people and make them understand that everyone loses when they participate in corrupt practices. By raising their level of awareness about the ills of corruption and the extent of damage that it does to the community, the people themselves will act to eliminate this practice once and for all. Public education must focus on making people realize that everybody has a stake in fighting corruption.

Educating the people can be done using many avenues—the formal education system, religious communities, mass media, or direct face-to-face contact. In India, schools are the targets of an

NGO's initiatives to promote moral and ethical education, whose curriculum includes good citizenship and democracy. In Cambodia, a group called "Transparency Task Force" has been formed, composing educators and anti-corruption pundits, which is developing a wide-ranging, counter-corruption curriculum, which will be adopted by the Ministry of Education in its formal educational program. It is based on putting forward traditional moral and ethical values that are advanced by Cambodian folk tales and Buddhist teachings.

In Australia, on the other hand, corruption education has mainly focused on training and educating civil servants and anticorruption practitioners. In 1998, the Australian National University introduced a course on Corruption and Anti-Corruption as part of its Masters Degree in Development Administration. By using its own anti-corruption agency as an example, the ANU course trains its students on identifying where corruption starts and develop strategies to reduce or eliminate corruption entirely.

The content and approach of each curriculum developed in these countries differ precisely because they are personalized to fit the culture and environment of its audience.

So it is important to educate every one in the world. Then only all the people in the world live happy. So "each one teach one" is necessary for now a days.

BIBLIOGRAPHY

1. "**Anti-Corruption Efforts in Africa**." U.S. Congress. House. Committee on International Relations. Hearing before the Subcommittee on Africa. 105th Congress, 2nd Session, 20 May 1998.
2. "**Bribery of Foreign Public Officials**." U.S. Congress. Senate. Committee on Foreign Relations. Hearing before the Committee on Foreign Relations. 105th Congress, 2nd Session, 9 June 1998.
3. '**The Old Testament Text'**, written by **Shemaryahu Talmon**, Professor of Bible, The Hebrew University of

Jerusalem, in The Cambridge History of the Bible, Cambridge, at the University Press, 1970, p. 159f.

4. A breach of syntax; any absurdity, impropriety or incongruity.
5. A Commentary on the HB, Ed The Rev. **J. R. Dummelow, NY, The Macmillan Co**, 1956, p. xiv.
6. A Commentary on the HB, Ed the Rev. **J. R. Dummelow, NY, The Macmillan Co**, 1956, p. xxiv.
7. A Commentary on the HB, Ed The Rev. **J. R. Dummelow, NY, The Macmillan Co**, 1956, pp. xxvii-xxix.
8. A defect in an eye, lens or mirror because of which rays from a single point do not focus on a single point.
9. **AAPAM** (1991). **Ethics and Accountability in African Public Services.** Report of the XIIIth round Table of the African Association for Public Administration and Management (AAPAM) held at Mababane, Swaziland, December 2-6.
10. **Ades, A**. and **Tella, R.D.** (1996). "The Causes and Consequences of Corruption: A Review of Recent Empirical Contributions" in Harris-White, B. and White, G. eds. Liberalization and the New Corruption. IDS Bulletin, Vol. 27, No. 2: 6-11.
11. **Adnan, S.** (1992). Flooding Patterns and Problems During 1991. Dhaka: Research and Advisory Services.
12. **Ahmed, B.** et al. (1992). "Government Malpractices", in **Report of the Task Forces on Bangladesh: Development Strategies for 1990s.** Vol.2, Dhaka: University Publishers Limited (UPL), pp.389-407.
13. **Ahmed. B**. et. at. (1992). "Government Malpractices" Report of the Task Forces on Bangladesh: Development Strategies for 1990s. Vol. 2. Dhaka: University Publishers Limited (UPL), pp. 389-407.
14. **Alam, M.S.** (1996). "Corruption in Administration" (in Bangla), **Bangla Bazar Patrika** (a vernacular daily newspaper) January 28 and 29.

15. **Alam, S.** (1990). Multiplex Thoughts. Dhaka: Bangladesh Cooperative Society Limited. Chapters 4 & 5.
16. **Alesina**, **Alberto** and **Beatrice Weder**. "Do Corrupt Governments Receive Less Foreign Aid?" American Economic Review vol. 92, no. 4; September 2002: pp. 1126-1137.
17. **Alfiler,** M.C.P. (1979). "Administrative Measures Against Bureaucratic Corruption: The Philippine Experience", **Philippine Journal of Public Administration (PJPA),** Vol.23, Nos.3 and 4: 321-349.
18. **Ali, A.** et. al eds. (1996). Development Issues of Bangladesh. Dhaka: UPL.
19. **Aminuzzaman, S.M**. (1996), " Accountability and Promotion of Ethics and Standard of Behaviour of the Public Bureaucracy in Bangladesh", Asian Review of Public Administration, Vol. 8. No. 1: 13-27.
20. **Aminuzzaman, S.M.** (1996). "Accountability and Promotion of Ethics and Standard of Behaviour of the Public Bureaucracy in Bangladesh", **Asian Review of Public Administration**, Vol.8, No.1: 13-27.
21. An original version of a MS from which a copy is produced.
22. **Androphy, Joel M. White-Collar Crime. St. Paul, Minn**.: West Group, 2001.
23. **Anechiarico, F. and Jacobs, J.B. (1996).** The Pursuit of Absolute Integrity: How Corruption Control Makes Government Ineffective. Chicago: The University of Chicago Press.
24. **Anticorruption Transition:** A Contribution to the Policy Debate. Washington, DC: International Bank for Reconstruction and Development and The World Bank, 2003.
25. **Arora, D. (1993).** "Conceptualizing the Context and Contextualising the Concept: Corruption Reconsidered", **Indian Journal of Public Administration (IJPA),** Vol.39, No.1: 1-19.

26. **Arora, D. (1993).** "Conceptualizing the Context and Contextualising the Concept: Corruption Reconsidered" Indian Journal of Public Administration (IJPA) Vol. 39, No. 1-19.

27. **Bailey, F Lee and Henry B. Rothblatt**. Defending Business and White-Collar Crime. Rochester, N.Y.: Lawyers Co-operative, 1984.

28. **Bardhan, Pranab (1997):** "Corruption and Development: A Review of Issues", Journal of Economic Literature, Vol. XXXV, No. September: 1320-1346.

29. **Behind the Corporate Veil**: Using Corporate Entities for Illicit Purposes. Paris: Organization for Economic Cooperation and Development, 2001.

30. **Blair, H. et al. (1992). The Bangladesh Democracy Program (BDP) Assessment: Final Report.** Washington, D.C.: Bureau for Private Enterprise, USAID.

31. **Blair, H.** et. al. (1992). The Bangladesh Democracy Program (BDP) Assessment: Final Report. Washington, DC: Bureau for Private Enterprise, USAID.

32. **Brademas, John,** and **Fritz Heimann**. "Tackling International Corruption: No Longer Taboo." Foreign Affairs vol. 77, no. 5; September-October 1998.

33. **Bruce M. Metzger**, The Text of the New Testament, Oxford at the Clarendon Press, 1964.

34. **Bruce M. Metzger**, The Text of the NT, Its Transmission, Corruption, and Restoration, Oxford at the Clarendon Press, 1964, pp. 186f.

35. **Bruce, W. (1995).** "Ideals and Conventions: Ethics for Public Administrators," Public Administration Review (PAR) Vol. 55, No. 1: 111-11 6.

36. **BUP (1997). Opinion Survey, 1997.** Dhaka: Bangladesh Unnayan Parishad (BUP).

37. **Caiden, G.E. (1991a).** "What Really is Public Maladministration?", **IJPA**, Vol.37, No.1:1-16.

38. **Caiden, G.E. (1991a).** Administrative Reform Comes of Age. New York: Walter de Gruyter.

39. **Caiden, G.E. (1991b).** "What Really is Public Maladministration?" IJPA, Vol. 37, No. 1.

40. **Caiden, G.E. (1991b). Administrative Reform Comes of Age**. New York: Walter de Gruyter.

41. **Caiden, G.E. (undated).** "Toward a General Theory of Official Corruption" Asian Journal of Public Administration.

42. **Caiden, G.E. and N. Caiden (1977).** "Administrative Corruption", **Public Administration Review**, Vol.37, No.3.

43. Caiden, G.E.(1988) . "Toward a General Theory of Official Corruption", **Asian Journal of Public Administration,** Vol.10, No.1: 3-26.

44. Carino, L.V. (1979). "The Definition of Graft and Corruption and the Conflict of Ethics and Law", **PJPA**, Vol.23, Nos 3 and 4:221-240.

45. **Carino, L.V. and R.P. Guzman (1979).** "Negative Bureaucratic Behaviour in the Philippines: The Final Report of the IDRC Philippine Team", **PJPA**, Vol.23, Nos.3 and 4:350-385.

46. Carpenter, Ted G. Bad Neighbor Policy: Washington's Futile War on Drugs in Latin America. New York: **Palgrave MacMillan, 2003**.

47. Center for International Private Enterprise. "Business Views on Combating Corruption." Economic Reform Today no. 2; 1998.

48. **Clarke, M. ed. (1983).** Corruption: Causes, Consequences and Control. London: Francis Pinter Ltd.

49. **Coleman, James W. The Criminal Elite**: Understanding White-Collar Crime. New York: Worth, 2002.

50. Corruption and Integrity: Best Business Practice in an Imperfect World. Washington, D.C.: Control Risks Group Limited, 1998.

51. **Davies, C.J. (1987).** "Controlling Administrative Corruption", Planning and Administration, Vol. 14, No. 2: 62-67.

52. **de Zwart, Frank (1994**): The Bureaucratic Merry-Go-Round: Manipulating the Transfer of Indian Civil Servants. Amsterdam: Amsterdam University Press.

53. **deLeon, Peter (1993):** Thinking about Political Corruption. Armonk, New York: M. E. Sharpe.

54. **Dininio, Phyllis, Sahr John Kpundeh, and Robert Leiken**. USAID Handbook for Fighting Corruption. Washington, D.C.: U.S. Agency for International Development, Center for Democracy and Governance, 1998.

55. **Doig, Alan (1984):** Corruption and Misconduct in Contemporary British Politics. Suffolk: Penguin Books.

56. **Doraiswamy, P. K. (1997):** "Tackling Corruption - Some Relevant, Difficult Issues", The Hindu, 05-08-98, pg.25, Col. a.

57. **Dummelow's** Commentary, op.cit., pp. xxvf.

58. **Dummelow's** Commentary, op.cit., pp. xxvif.

59. **Dwivedi, O.P. (1995).** "Reflections on Moral Government and Public Service as a Vocation" IJPA, Vol. 41, No. 3: 296-306.

60. **Dwivedi, S.N. and G.S. Bhargava (1967). Political Corruption in India.** New Delhi: Popular Book House.

61. **Elliot, Kimberly Ann**, ed. Corruption and the Global Economy. Washington, D.C.: Institute for International Economics, 1997.

62. **Franda, M. (1982). Bangladesh: The First Decade**. New Delhi: South Asian.

63. **Franda, M. (1982).** Bangladesh: The First Decade. New Delhi: South Asian.

64. **Gantz, David A.** "The Foreign Corrupt Practices Act: Professional and Ethical Challenges for Lawyers." Arizona Journal of International and Comparative Law 1997.

65. **Geddes MacGregor,** 'The Bible in the Making' London, John Murray, 1961, p.9f.

66. **Gilman, S.G. and Lewis, C.W. (1996).** "Public Service Ethics: A Global Dialogue" Public Administration Review (PAR), Vol. 56, No. 6: 517-524.

67. **Goudie, A.W. and D. Stasange (1979). Corruption: The Issues.** OECD Development Centre Technical Paper No.122. Paris: Organization for Economic Cooperation and Development.

68. **Goudie, A.W. and Stasange, D. (1997).** Corruption: The Issues. OECD Development Centre Technical Paper No. 122. Paris: Organization for Economic Cooperation and Development (OECD).

69. **Gouhan, S. and Paul S. eds. (1997).** Corruption in India: Agenda for Action. New Delhi: Vision Books.

70. **Gouhan, S. and S. Paul (1997). Corruption in India: Agenda for Action**. New Delhi: Vision Books.

71. Gould, D.J. (1980). **Bureaucratic Corruption and Underdevelopment in the Third World: The Case of Zaire.** New York: Pergaman.

72. **Gould, D.J. (1991).** "Administrative Corruption: Incidence, Causes, and Remedial Strategies in A. Farazmand ed. **Handbook of Comparative and Development Public Administration.** New York: Marcel Dekker, Inc., pp.467-480.

73. **Gould, D.J. (1991).** "Administrative Corruption: Incidence, Causes and Remedial Strategies" in A. Farazmand ed. Handbook of Comparative and Development Public Administration. New York: Marcel Dekker, Inc, pp. 467-480

74. **Gould, D.J. and Amaro-Reyes, J. A. (1985).** The Effects of Corruption on Administrative Performance: Illustrations from Developing Countries. World Bank Staff Paper No. 580. Washington, D.C.: The World Bank.

75. **Gould, D.J. and J.A. Amaro-Reyes (1985). The Effects of Corruption on Administrative Performance: Illustrations from Developing Countries.** World Bank Staff Paper No.580. Washington, DC.: The World Bank.

76. **Gupta, Akhil (1995):** "Blurred Boundaries: The Discourse of Corruption, the Culture of Politics, and the Imagined State", American Ethnologist, Vol. 22, No. 2: 375-402.

77. **Gupta, Sanjeev, Hamid Davoodi, and Rosa Alonso-Terme**. Does Corruption Affect Income Inequality and Poverty? Washington, DC: International Monetary Fund, 1998.

78. **Harriss-White, B. and G. White (1996).** "Editorial Introduction: Corruption, Liberalization and Democracy", in B. Harris-White and G. White eds. **Liberalization and the New Corruption,** Vol.27, No.2: 1-5.

79. **Harriss-White, Barbara & White, Gordon (1996):** "Corruption, Liberalization and Democracy: Editorial Introduction", IDS Bulletin: Liberalization and the New Corruption, Vol. 27, No. 2: 1-5.

80. **Harris-White, Barbara (1996):** "Liberalization and Corruption: Resolving the Paradox (A Discussion Based on South Indian Material)", IDS Bulletin: Liberalization and the New Corruption, Vol. 27, No. 2: 31-39.

81. **Heidenheimer, A. J., Heclo, H. & Adams, C. T. (1990):** Comparative Public Policy: The Politics of Social Choice in America, Europe and Japan. New York: St. Martin's Press.

82. **Hotchkiss, Carolyn**. "The Sleeping Dog Stirs: New Signs of Life in Efforts to End Corruption in International Business." Journal of Public Policy and Marketing vol. 17, no. 1; Spring 1998.

83. **Howell, Llewellyn D.** "Corruption and Crisis in the Global Economy." USA Today vol. 126, no. 2636; May 1, 1998.

84. **Husain, S. (1988).** Corruption in Public Offices: Some Conceptual Issues in the Context of Bangladesh. Kotbari, Comilla: Bangladesh Academy for Rural Development (BARD). ie. The very word.

85. **J. Philip Hyatt,** in The Enc. Americana, op.cit, pp. 659-662.
86. **J. Philip Hyatt**, Vanderbilt University's article 'Textual Criticism of the OT' in The Encyclopedia Americana, Grolier Incorporated, Vol.3, 1984, p. 658.
87. **Kaufmann, Daniel**. "Corruption: The Facts." Foreign Policy no. 107; Summer 1997.
88. **Khan, M.M. (1979). Administrative Reform in Bangladesh.** New Delhi: South Asian.
89. **Khan, M.M. (1989a).** "Resistance to Administrative Reform in Bangladesh, 1972-1987", Public Administration and Development, Vol. 9, No.3: 301-314.
90. **Khan, M.M. (1989a).** "The Electoral Process in Bangladesh", **Regional Studies,** Vol.7, No.3: 95-111.
91. **Khan, M.M. (1989b).** "Resistance to Administrative Reform in Bangladesh, 1972-1987", **Public Administration and Development (PAD),** Vol. 9, No.3: 301-314.
92. **Khan, M.M. (1997a).** "Bureaucratic Culture in Bangladesh" in Khan, M. M. Administrative Reforms in Bangladesh. New Delhi: South Asian.
93. **Khan, M.M. (1997b).** "Unions in Bangladesh: An Overview", paper presented in the 17th World Congress of International Political Science Association (IPSA) held in Seoul, Korea on August 17-21.
94. **Khan, M.M. and H.M. Zafarullah (1979).** "The 1979 Parliamentary Elections in Bangladesh", **Asian Survey,** Vol.19, No.10: 1023-1036.
95. **Khan, M.M. and Zafarullah, H.M. (1979).** "The 1979 Parliamentary Elections in Bangladesh," Asian Survey, Vol. 19, No. 10: 1023 -1036.
96. **Khan, M.M. et al. (1995).** "Ethics and Public Service in Bangladesh', **IJPA**, Vol.41, No.3:592-608.
97. **Khan, M.M. et. al. (1995).** "Ethics and Public Service in Bangladesh", Indian Journal of Public Administration, Vol. 41, No. 3: 592-608.

98. **Khan, Mushtaq H. (1996):** "A Typology of Corrupt Transactions in Developing Countries", IDS Bulletin: Liberalization and the New Corruption, Vol. 27, No. 2: 12-21.

99. **Khan, Mushtaq H. (1996**): "The Efficiency Implications of Corruption", Journal of International Development, Vol. 8, No. 5: 683-696.

100. **Kidd, John and Frank-Jurgen Richter**, eds. Fighting Corruption in Asia: Causes, Effects and Remedies. River Edge, NJ: World Scientific, 2003.

101. **Kjellberg, F. (1992):** "Corruption as an Analytical Problem: Some Notes on Research on Public Corruption", Indian Journal of Administrative Science, Vol. III, No. 2: 195-221.

102. **Klitgaard, R. (1988). Controlling Corruption.** Berkeley, C.A.:University of California Press.

103. **Klitgaard, Robert**. "International Cooperation Against Corruption." Finance and Development vol. 35, no. 1; March 1998.

104. **Kochanek, S.A. (1993). Patron-Client Politics and Business in Bangladesh**. Dhaka: UPL.

105. **Kochanek, S.A. (1993).** Patron-Client Politics and Business in Bangladesh. Dhaka: UPL, 1993.

106. **Kong, tat Yan (1996):** "Corruption and its Institutional Foundations: The Experience of South Korea", IDS Bulletin: Liberalization and the New Corruption, Vol. 27, No. 2: 48-55.

107. **Kpundeh, Sahr J., and Irene Hors,** eds. Corruption and Integrity Improvement Initiatives in Developing Countries. New York: United Nations.

108. **Kramer, J.J. (1997).** "Political Corruption in Post-Communist Russia: The Case for Democratization", paper presented at the XVIIth World Congress of International Political Science Association (IPSA) held in Seoul, Korea on August 17-21.

109. **Kramer, J.M. (1997).** "Political Corruption in Post-Communist Russia: The Case for Democratization", paper presented at the 17th World Congress of International Political Science Association (IPSA) held in Seoul, Korea on August 17-21.

110. **Leff, H.N. (1979**). "Economic Development through Bureaucratic Corruption" in M.U. Ekpo ed. **Bureaucratic Corruption in Sub-Saharan Africa: Toward a Search for Causes and Consequences.** Washington, D.C.: University Press of America.

111. **Lewis, D.J. (1996). Corruption in Bangladesh: Discourse, Judgments and Modalities.** CDS Occasional Paper No.5. Bath: Centre for Development Studies.

112. **Lewis, D.J. (1996).** Corruption in Bangladesh: Discourse, Judgments and Modalities. CDS Occasional Paper No 5. Bath: Centre for Development Studies, University of Bath.

113. **Leys, C. (1970).** "What is the Problem about Corruption?" in A.J. Heidenheimer ed. **Political Corruption: Readings in Comparative Perspective**. New York: Holt, Rinehart and Winston.

114. **Little, Walter (1996):** "Corruption and Democracy in Latin America", IDS Bulletin: Liberalization and the New Corruption, Vol. 27, No. 2: 64-70.

115. **Lo, T. W. (1993).** Corruption and Politics in Hong Kong and China. Buckingham: Open University Press.

116. **Lo, T.W. (1993). Corruption and Politics in Hong Kong and China.** Buckingham: Open University Press.

117. **Lozada, Carlos**. "Corruption's True Face." Foreign Policy May/June 2002.

118. **M.M. Khan (1989b).** "The Electoral Process in Bangladesh," Regional Studies Vol. 7, No.3: 95 - 111.

119. **Maloney, C. (1986). Behaviour and Poverty in Bangladesh.** Dhaka: UPL.

120. **Maniruzzaman, T. (1982)**. **Group Interests and Political Changes: Studies of Pakistan and Bangladesh**. New Delhi: South Asian.

121. **Maniruzzaman, T. (1982).** Group Interests and Political Changes: Studies of Pakistan and Bangladesh. New Delhi: South Asian.**Martin, A. Timothy**. "Corruption and Improper Payments: Global Trends and Applicable Laws." The Alberta Law Review 1998.

122. **Masutha, J. and Kotze, H. (1997).** "Political Corruption in South Africa: An Analysis of Elite Perceptions", paper presented at the 17th World Congress of IPSA held in Seoul, Korea on August 17-21.

123. **Mauro, Paolo**. "Corruption: Causes, Consequences, and Agenda for Further Research." Finance and Development vol. 35, no. 1; March 1998.

124. **Mauro, Paolo**. The Effects of Corruption on Growth, Investment, and Government Expenditure. Washington: International Monetary Fund, 1996.

125. **Mauro, Paolo**. Why Worry About Corruption? Washington: International Monetary Fund, 1997.

126. **Mustafa, S. (1997).** "Corruption Costs Millions, says UNDP", **Financial Express** July, 31.

127. New Perspectives on Combating Corruption. Washington, DC: Transparency International and International Bank for Reconstruction and Development, 1998.

128. No Longer Business as Usual: Fighting Bribery and Corruption. Paris: Organization for Economic Cooperation and Development, 2000.

129. **Nye, J.S. (1979).** "Corruption and Political Development: A Cost-Benefit Analysis" in M.U. Ekpo ed. **Bureaucratic Corruption in Sub-Saharan Africa: Toward a Search for Causes and Consequences**. Washington, D.C.: University Press of America.

130. **Ofosu-Amaah, W. Paatii, Raj Soopramanien**, and **Kishor Uprety**. Combating Corruption: A Comparative Review of Selected Legal Aspects of State Practice and International Initiatives. Washington: World Bank Institute, 1999.

131. **Oppenheimer, Andres. Blindfolded**: The United States and the Business of Corruption in Latin America. Buenos Aires: Editorial Sudamericana, 2001.

132. **Ouma, O.A. (1991).** "Corruption in Public Policy and its Impact on Development: The Case of Uganda since 1979", **PAD**, Vol.11, No.5: 473-489.

133. **Ouma, S.O.A. (1991).** "Corruption in Public Policy and Its Impact on Development: The Case of Uganda Since 1979", Public Administration and Development (PAD), Vol. 11, No. 5: 473-489.

134. **Padhay, K.S. (1986). Corruption in Politics: A Case Study**. Delhi: B.R. Publishing Corporation.

135. **Padhy, K.S. (1986).** Corruption in Politics: A Case Study. Delhi: B.R. Publishing Corporation.

136. **Paul, S. (1979a).** "Corruption: Who Will Bell the Cat?", **Economic and Political Weekly** June, 7:1350-1355.

137. **Paul, S. (1979b).** "Corruption in India: A Strategic Agenda for Action" in S. Guhan and S. Paul eds. **Corruption in India: Agenda for Action.** New Delhi: Vision Books, pp.286-304.

138. **Paul, S. (1997).** "Corruption: Who Will Bell the Cat?" Economic and Political Weekly June 7,: 1350-1355.

139. **Paul, Samuel (1997):** "Corruption: Who Will Bell the Cat?", Economic and Political Weekly, Vol. 32, No. 23: 1350-1355.

140. **Pavarala, V. (1996). Interpreting Corruption: Elite Perspectives in India**. New Delhi: Sage.

141. **Pavarala, V. (1996).** Interpreting Corruption: Elite Perspectives in India. New Delhi: Sage.

142. **Pavarala, V. (1996):** Interpreting Corruption: Elite Perspectives in India. New Delhi: SAGE Publications.

143. **Peake's** Commentary on the Bible, OT Ed H. H. Rowley, Thomas Nelson & Sons Ltd, London, 1967, p. 75.

144. **Podgor, Ellen S. and Jerold H. Israel**. White-Collar Crime In A Nutshell. St. Paul, Minn.: West, 1997.

145. **Poole-Robb, Stuart**. Risky Business: Corruption, Fraud, Terrorism and Other Threats to Global Business. London: Kogan Page, 2002.

146. **Pope, J. (1996).** "National Integrity Programs" in P. Lengseth and K. Galt eds. **Partnership for Governance**. Proceedings of a Conference held in Copenhagen on May, 31, pp.23-26.

147. **Prof. Dr. Geddes MacGregor**, Dean of the Graduate School of Religion and Professor of Philosophical Theology in the University of Southern California, John Murray, Albemarle Street London, 1961, pp. 8f.

148. **Qayyum, Ayesha**. "New Anti-Bribery Treaty Analyzed." International Commercial Litigation no. 28; March 1998.

149. **Quah, J.S.T. (1989).** "Singapore's Experience in Curbing Corruption" in A.J. Heidenheimer, et al.eds. **Political Corruption: A Handbook**. New Brunswick: Transaction Publishers, pp.841-853.

150. **Quah, J.S.T. (1995).** "Sustaining Quality in the Singapore Civil Service" in **Government in Transition**. London: Commonwealth Secretariat, pp.147-157.

151. **Rahman, M.A**. et al. (1993). **Towards Better Government in Bangladesh**. Dhaka: Bangladesh Government Press.

152. **Rahman, M.A**. et. al. (1993). Towards Better Government in Bangladesh. Dhaka: Bangladesh Government Press, pp. 71-82.

153. **Rahman, M.H. (1994).** "Corruption and Patronage: The Social and Political Linkage" in M.H. Rahman, **Decentralisation and Rural Society in Bangladesh: A Study of Bureaucratic Constraints on Access in the Upazila Structure.** Unpublished Ph.D. Thesis. Swansea: Centre for Development Studies, University College of Swansea, University of Wales.

154. **Rahman, M.H. (1994).** "Corruption and Patronage: The Social and Political Linkage" in Rahman, M.H. Decentralisation and Rural Society in Bangladesh: A Study

of Bureaucratic Constraints on Access in the Upazilla Structure. Unpublished Ph.D. Thesis. Swansea: Centre for Development Studies, University College of Swansea, University of Wales.

155. **Rahman, M.S. (1991).** Administrative Elite in Bangladesh. New Delhi: Manak Publishers.

156. **Rogow, A.A. and H.D. Laswell (1970).** "The Definition of Corruption" in A.J. Heidenheimer ed. **Political Corruption: Readings in Comparative Analysis**. New York: Holt, Rinehart and Winstan.

157. **Sanghi, V.K.C.(1996).** "Deterring Corruption in Public Purchase: Need for Mandatory Price Negotiation Approach," IJPA, Vol. 42, No. 2: 153-166.

158. **Sangita, S. N. (1995).** "Institutional Arrangement for Controlling Corruption in Public Life: Karnataka Experience" IJPA, Vol. 41, No. 1: 45-67

159. **Sarkar, J.N. (1935). Mughal Administration**. Calcutta: M.C. Sarkar and Sons Limited.

160. **Scott, J.C. (1972). Comparative Political Corruption**. Englewood Cliffs, N.J.: Princeton Hall, Inc.

161. Septuagint means seventy commonly written as LXX. It was the Greek translation of the OT of the Bible made by almost seventy or seventy two scholars in Alexandria during the 3rd and 2nd centuries BC.

162. **Sherman, Mark**. White-Collar Crime. Washington, D.C.: Federal Judicial Center, 2001.

163. **Siddiquee, N.A. (1997).** "Politics and Administration at the Upazilla Level: Problems of Access and Participation" in Siddiquee, N.A. Decentralisation and Development: Theory and Practice in Bangladesh. Dhaka: University of Dhaka.

164. **Siddiquee, N.A. (1997). Decentralisation and Development Theory and Practice in Bangladesh**. Dhaka: University of Dhaka.

165. **Siddiqui, K. (1996).** "On Combating Corruption" in Siddique, K. Towards Good Governance in Bangladesh. Dhaka: UPL, pp. 22-26.

166. **Siddiqui, K.et al. (1990). Social Formation in Dhaka City: A Study in Third World Urban Sociology.** Dhaka: UPL.

167. **Sidel, John T. (1996):** "Siam and its Twin? Democratization and Bossism in Contemporary Thailand and the Philippines", IDS Bulletin: Liberalization and the New Corruption, Vol. 27, No. 2: 56-63.

168. **Soto, Hernando de**. The Other Path: The Economic Answer to Terrorism. New York: Basic Books, 2002.

169. **Stahl, O.G. (1994).** Ethical Foundation." in A. Farazmand ed. Handbook of Bureaucracy. New York: Marcel Dekker, Inc, pp. 295-303.

170. **Stapenhurst, Rick, and Sahr J. Kpundeh**, eds. Curbing Corruption: Toward a Model for Building National Integrity. Washington: World Bank Institute, 1999.

171. **Tanzi, Vito**, and **Hamid Davoodi.** Roads to Nowhere: How Corruption in Public Investment Hurts Growth. Washington: International Monetary Fund, 1998

172. **Taslim, M.A. (1994).** "Public Corruption, External Interference and Policy Making in a Dependent Regime" in H.M. Zafarullah et al. eds. **Policy Issues in Bangladesh.** New Delhi: South Asian, pp.291-307.

173. **Taslim, M.A. (1994).** "Public Corruption, External Interference and Policy Making in a Dependent Regime" in Zafarullah, H.M. et. al. eds. Policy Issues in Bangladesh. New Delhi: South Asian, pp. 296-306.

174. **Thakur, U. (1979). Corruption in Ancient India**. New Delhi: Abhinav Publications.

175. **Thakur, U. (1979).** Corruption in Ancient India. New Delhi: Abhinav Publications.

176. The World Bank and Anticorruption in Europe and Central Asia: Enhancing Transparency, Voice and Accountability. Washington, DC: International Bank for Reconstruction and Development and The World Bank, 2003.

177. **Theobald, R. (1990). Corruption Development and Underdevelopment.** London: Macmillan.

178. **Theobald, R. (1990).** Corruption, Development and Underdevelopment. London: Macmillan.

179. **Tilman, R.O. (1970).** "Black Market Bureaucracy" in A.J. Heidenheimer ed. **Political Corruption: Readings in Comparative Analysis.** New York: Holt, Renehart and Winston.

180. **Tulchin, Joseph S., and Ralph H. Espach**, eds. Combatting Corruption in Latin America. Washington, DC: Woodrow Wilson Center, 2000.

181. **Uncial**, i.e. written in majuscule (large letters) writing with rounded un-joined letters found in manuscripts of the 4th-8th century, from which modern capitals are derived.

182. **UNDP (1993). Report on Public Administration Sector Study in Bangladesh.** New York: United Nations Development Programme (UNDP).

183. **United Nations (1990). Corruption in Government.** Report of an Interregional Seminar held in The Haque, The Netherlands on December 11-15. New York: The United Nations.

184. **Vine, T.L.V. (1975). Political Corruption: The Ghana Case.** Stanford, CA: Hoover Institution.

185. **Vine, T.L.V. (1975).** Political Corruption: The Ghana Case. Stanford, CA: Hoover Institution.

186. **Vogl, Frank**. "The Supply Side of Global Bribery." Finance and Development vol. 35, no. 2; June 1998.

187. **Wade, Robert (1982):** The System of Administrative and Political Corruption: Canal Irrigation in South India. The Journal of Development Studies, 1982.

188. **Wade, Robert (1985):** The Market for Public Office: Why the Indian State is not Better at Development. World Development.

189. Walsh, James. "A World War on Bribery." Time International June 22, 1998.

190. **Wart, M.V. (1996)."**The Sources of Ethical Decision Making for Individuals in the Public Sector," PAR, Vol.56, No.6: 525-523.

191. **White, Gordon (1996):** “Corruption and Market Reform in China”, IDS Bulletin: Liberalization and the New Corruption, Vol. 27, No. 2: 40-47.

192. **White-Harris, B. and White, G. eds. (1996).** Liberalization and the New Corruption. IDS Bulletin, Vol. 27, No. 2. Brighton: Institute of Development Studies, University of Sussex.

193. **Wilmhurst, J. (1995).** “Political, Economic and Administrative Reforms to Promote Good Governance,” paper presented to the International Symposium on Corruption and Good Government.

194. World Bank (1996a). **Bangladesh: Government That Works: Reforming the Public Sector.** Washington, DC: The World Bank.

195. World Bank (1996b). **Bangladesh: An Agenda for Action.** Washington, DC: The World Bank.

196. World Bank, The (1996). Bangladesh: Government That Works: Reforming the Public Sector. Dhaka: UPL, pp. 66-71.

APPENDIX-A

English Version of the Attitude Scale Towards Corruption

S.No.	Statements	SA	A	D	DA	SDA
1.	Corruption is obstacle for development.	( )	( )	( )	( )	( )
2.	Every where there is Corruption.	( )	( )	( )	( )	( )
3.	The cause of Corruption is poverty.	( )	( )	( )	( )	( )
4.	The cause of Corruption is the aspiration of comfortable life.	( )	( )	( )	( )	( )
5.	By knowing the corruption character of the person can be assessed.	( )	( )	( )	( )	( )
6.	The Corrupted people number is very few.	( )	( )	( )	( )	( )
7.	The Corruption politicians are very few.	( )	( )	( )	( )	( )
8.	It is very difficult to control Corruption.	( )	( )	( )	( )	( )
9.	Corrupted officers and politicians must be questioned.	( )	( )	( )	( )	( )
10.	Without Corruption there is no evelopment.	( )	( )	( )	( )	( )
11.	Corruption in India is very low.	( )	( )	( )	( )	( )

12. Corrupted people must be encouraged. ( ) ( ) ( ) ( ) ( )
13. There must be lessons about corruption ( ) ( ) ( ) ( ) ( ) in the test books.
14. It is not advisable to fight unitedly against ( ) ( ) ( ) ( ) ( ) Corruption.
15. Corruption is very high in Revenue ( ) ( ) ( ) ( ) ( ) Department.
16. No chance for Corruption in Educational ( ) ( ) ( ) ( ) ( ) Institutions.
17. Corruption can be reduced by increasing ( ) ( ) ( ) ( ) ( ) the literacy percentage.
18. If selfishness increases then corruption ( ) ( ) ( ) ( ) ( ) decreases.
19. Women have to participate actively in all ( ) ( ) ( ) ( ) ( ) sectors of life for decreasing corruption.
20. If more powers are delegated to women, ( ) ( ) ( ) ( ) ( ) then corruption can be decreased.
21. The Anti-corruption agencies should ( ) ( ) ( ) ( ) ( ) be increased.
22. The Government can't taking proper ( ) ( ) ( ) ( ) ( ) steps to control corruption.
23. Loksatha trying to control Corruption. ( ) ( ) ( ) ( ) ( )
24. People come voluntarily to control ( ) ( ) ( ) ( ) ( ) Corruption.
25. If more powers are given to rich people ( ) ( ) ( ) ( ) ( ) then India will become Anti-corrupted country.
26. If the awareness of student about ( ) ( ) ( ) ( ) ( ) Corruption increases, then Corruption will be decreased in the future.
27. Suggestions of Educated and Social ( ) ( ) ( ) ( ) ( ) Workers should be taken for controlling Corruption.
28. Corruption decreases when helping ( ) ( ) ( ) ( ) ( ) nature increases.

29. There is no Corruption in Irrigation ( ) ( ) ( ) ( ) ( ) department.
30. Severe punishment may be given to the ( ) ( ) ( ) ( ) ( ) Corrupted people.
31. Administrative reforms are not necessary ( ) ( ) ( ) ( ) ( ) for controlling Corruption.
32. If Corruption is not controlled, then the ( ) ( ) ( ) ( ) ( ) violence will be increased.
33. If we want Anti-corrupted country then ( ) ( ) ( ) ( ) ( ) elect best leaders.
34. It is necessary to take steps against ( ) ( ) ( ) ( ) ( ) Corruption on war footing.
35. The concentrating actively in controlling ( ) ( ) ( ) ( ) ( ) of corruption.
36. Now a days even I.A.S. officers are also ( ) ( ) ( ) ( ) ( ) trying for Corruption.
37. The Police department successful in ( ) ( ) ( ) ( ) ( ) controlling the Corruption.
38. There is no proper Judicial system to ( ) ( ) ( ) ( ) ( ) control Corruption.
39. Corruption is very high in educated ( ) ( ) ( ) ( ) ( ) persons.
40. The poor becoming very poor because ( ) ( ) ( ) ( ) ( ) of Corruption in the country.
41. All lived happly with un-controlled ( ) ( ) ( ) ( ) ( ) Corruption.
42. To control Corruption it is necessary for ( ) ( ) ( ) ( ) ( ) the establishing separate ministry.
43. The student unions should make ( ) ( ) ( ) ( ) ( ) necessary trials for controlling the corruption.
44. Parents should tell about corruption to their ( ) ( ) ( ) ( ) ( ) children.
45. Nobody is deceived by Corruption in ( ) ( ) ( ) ( ) ( ) his/her life.

46. Social reformers are not concentrating on ( ) ( ) ( ) ( ) ( )
    Corruption.
47. The present circumstances can't co-operate ( ) ( ) ( ) ( ) ( )
    for Anti-corruption.
48. Corruption is decreasing day by day. ( ) ( ) ( ) ( ) ( )
49. The politicians are trying to control ( ) ( ) ( ) ( ) ( )
    Corruption with all their efforts.
50. The Corruption will be controlled with in a ( ) ( ) ( ) ( ) ( )
    month.
51. Corrupted people should not be elected for ( ) ( ) ( ) ( ) ( )
    the Assembly and the Parliament.
52. The Government should give encouragement ( ) ( ) ( ) ( ) ( )
    for Anti-corruption agencies.
53. The Teacher's role is very important in ( ) ( ) ( ) ( ) ( )
    controlling the Corruption.
54. There is a need for change in Educational ( ) ( ) ( ) ( ) ( )
    system for controlling the Corruption.
55. Corruption will disappear, if every person ( ) ( ) ( ) ( ) ( )
    in the country strives for the development
    of the country.
56. Seminars will be conducted in the educational ( ) ( ) ( ) ( ) ( )
    institutions to know about corruption.
57. The Authors of the books and journals have ( ) ( ) ( ) ( ) ( )
    not made constructive criticism about
    corruption.
58. Corruption decreases, when the number of ( ) ( ) ( ) ( ) ( )
    Ideal families increases.
59. If we respect the constitution and its ( ) ( ) ( ) ( ) ( )
    amendments, then there is no Corruption.
60. Awareness programs about Corruption and ( ) ( ) ( ) ( ) ( )
    its evil effects have to arranged for every citizen.
61. The Government Anti-corruption department ( ) ( ) ( ) ( ) ( )
    officers themselves are involving in
    Corruption activities.

62. The State Government is not taking plangent ( ) ( ) ( ) ( ) ( ) measures on the people trying to involve in corruption activities.
63. The number of Anti-corruption bureaus ( ) ( ) ( ) ( ) ( ) should be increased.

2. Invariable Fears of Teachers

1

Introduction

Stress has been acknowledged inherent in the process of teaching. Most teachers, howsoever bright, well read, experienced and well prepared experience some amount of stress while going to lecture in front of the student, but manage to handle it. It is also true that some feel more stressed than others and face occasional difficulty in coping with it. Some teachers find it quite heavy on them and extremely difficult carry on the work, as they are not able to either structure the work environment or exercise control over the factors underlying the stress, or to enhance their capability to cope. It then threatens to adversely impact their physical health reduces their teaching commitment and effectiveness to the extent of their needing professional help. Prolonged periods of intense stress, if not taken care of, can produce feelings of emotional exhaustion, reduce personal accomplishment, induce a sense of professional failure, and even a tendency to act with the clientele in a depersonalised manner, the symptoms which define burnout. Stress and burnout among teachers found directly influence their functioning and survival in the system, and quality of educational and related services offered to all students, and without exception for those with special needs.

STRESS AND BURNOUT IN INDIAN CONTEXT

As stated in the introduction and other subsequent places in the book, although the definitional complexities in the assessment of stress and burnout are enormous and difficult to be resolved in general. An additional problem has been confronted by researchers in the understanding and assessment of stress and burnout in educational institutions of south Asia because of the specific cultural values of obedience of authority, nurturance of the young, etc. The socio-cultural situations have though, undergone gradual changes in the post independence period, and the difficulty of such unmet unconditional expectations now characterize the numerous interpersonal problems at all levels from administrative heads to students. The emotional strains of interpersonal emotional distances and the non-reciprocal relationships among different sections often operate at the latent level, and camouflage the severity of stress effects.

Like many of the educational institutions in south Asia, teachers in contemporary Indian schools are confronted with the reality of diverse social groups of educators and pupils, large size of class and raised expectations, leaving for them little scope and time for personal interaction with students and colleagues. Over the years, as social power and money have become important personal and social values, and the new professions have emerged, the teaching profession has got devalued. Teachers do not have the desired social respect, nor do they get adequate financial rewards/support for their work. Teachers expected to confer knowledge, and make every child the best achiever in every domain of activity. The task is challenging and demanding, but the teachers represent a mixed lot, with varied levels of skills, capabilities, resources, etc. Teachers who are capability and good, generally respected and appreciated, but instances are uncommon, when parents and students alike so not give a hot to the teachers, and blame them for any shortcomings observed in children/ school. Many parents do not wish their child to be a teacher. Many (parents, husbands and in-laws) view teaching as an ideal profession for women, as they can finish their work by the afternoon and take care of their home and children (a part time employee on full salary).

There has been little research in the Indian schools in areas of teacher concerns, stress and burnout. The first and School Surveys of Research in Education (Buch, 1974, 1979) did not include any study on teacher stress and burnout. A later bibliography (Dave and Murry, 1933) included three studies, each emphasizing a different aspect of burnout. As the pressures to perform from various quarters continue to rise, despite the adverse conditions of functioning of teaching institutions, teachers need familial and social support in differentiating across variety of stresses and in handling the day to day stresses, and thus prevent burnout.

INTRODUCTION: SETTING THE SCENE

Stress, burnout and coping researches have been confining for years to clinical areas, and the terms have acquired negative connotations, with which the inflicted struggled in a bid to find relief, and in the process depleted and/or exhausted the resources under their control. This indicates an unquestionable acceptance of the underlying assumption of persons going through the stressful experiences, having no control/volition or an alternative path out, and thus the need of therapy. The common experience as well as the evidence from research does not validate it. There neither is adequate logical ground to argue and suggest that all types of stress are necessarily negative and unhealthy for ones functioning, nor are the stress and burnout equivalents. A distinction been made in the literature between positive and negative stress, and between stress and burnout. Positive stress called eustress, and negative stress labelled distress. In fact, the positive affect has not been entirely neglected in the classical models of stress either. It has been discussed in relation to the (a) primary appraisal of stressful situations as challenges, which signal the probability of makings gains and characterized by positive emotions, like eagerness, excitement, and confidence. (b) Appraisal of the resolution of a stressful encounter as successful leading to emotions of happiness and pride. (c) Cessation of aversive conditions, when people are likely to experience an offsetting positive emotion, such as relief, and (d) Examining of the other positive outcomes of stressful events, even if the events have not been favorably resolved. The positive outcomes may include perceived benefits of stressful encounters, newly acquired skills and resources that may help in coping, and spiritual/ religious transformation in thinking and attitudes.

MEANING OF STRESS

Stress is a condition stream on ones emotions, thought processes and physical conditions. When it is excessive, it can pretend once ability to cope with environment. (Hans Selye, 1976) “Stress is the general term applied to the pressures; employs developed various symptoms of stress as, “an adjective demand placed on the organism”.

From the above definitions, it may understand that stress pretends the wellbeing of the organism; conditions that tend to because stress called pressure. In this age of anxiety, stress considered as an inevitable aspect of human life, forcing him to cope up with it for successful and happy life. The main factors of creating stress in individual are Biological, Psychological and Socio-Cultural. Biological factors influence all aspects of our behavior including our intellectual capabilities, basic temperament, primary reaction tendencies and stress tolerance. Psychosocial factors of stress also influence the well-being of the individual in contemporary life. Stress due to failure, losses, personal limitations, guilt and loneliness leads to self-deviation. Modern living is a bundle load of pressures acting on individuals. Each individual experience his own unique pattern of pressures such as competing with others, meeting educational, occupational, and marital depends and coping with the complexity and in rapid pace of modern life . There are other socio-cultural factors creating stress on modern man such as problems of war and violence, group prejudice and discrimination, economic and unemployment problems, rapid social change existential anxiety.

JOB STRESS

In this last decade of twentieth century, many people are unable to cope up with stress generated because of circumstances forcing them to adopt fact-paced life styles. This position is highly significant when people are at work. A rational and logical inference one can make, now basing on the above premises is that working styles are also subjected to change in accordance to the fast changing life styles, mat be a presupposition for work stress or job stress. Therefore, job stress has received an increasing concern to the researchers in the areas of organizational behavior and social psychology, who have been undertaking evidences about the effects of stress on the organization, worker output, and the physical and emotional well-being of the worker.

TEACHERS STRESS

Job stress is the most common psychological phenomena that are prevalent among people who are in different jobs and professions. The stress studies are initially directed toward industrial organization. With the private sector. Researchers have come to believe that stress may be especially prevalent among human service professions, particularly the teaching profession, (Kryacou and Suteliffe 1977-78; Pettigrew and Wolf 1982, Cherniss 1980; and Cooper and Marshall 1980). As teaching is a human service profession, stress with in the teaching profession is considerable and may have far-reaching consequences on the entire education system. Teaching is a complex process were in teacher is expected to exhibit many skills. This makes a teacher to experience stress in the profession.

Further Pettergrew and Wolf (1982) opined, "Teacher stress has a Nation-wide concern and relatively new area of empirical research". Concerns regarding stress among schoolteacher have been raised for over 40 years (Tunk, Meeks and Turk 1982) stress is considered very significant in any educative process much attention is not drawn towards this. Teacher behavior and his performance, classroom interactions, school and classroom climate may consider as the important components of any educative process.

It is not easy to ascertain sources of teacher stress, as its ambit is unlimited. However, several attempts are made to identify the sources that possible, create stress among teachers. Factors prepared by teachers as being troublesome or stressful have included students displine, negative student attitudes towards school, physical violence, is adequate preparation time, lack of clear role definition and heavy workloads".(Bearly, Myette and serna, 1983;Chichen and Koff, 1978;Gollady and Noel 1978;Olanderand Ferrel, 1970).

Further Kaiser and Polezynsky (1982) identified factors within educators themselves as a potential source of excess stress. Quick and Quick (1979) proposed four groups of factors creating work stress. They are 1) Role factors, 2) Job factors, 3) Physical factors and 4) Interpersonal factors. A heap of literature available on job stress identified main sources such as job setting, organizational, situational, lack of control over work, co-workers etc.

Teacher is subjected to stress due to incoherent social life, widening social distance, segregation, lack of social support, corruption, nepotism, unnecessary societal involvement in day-to-day activities, high degree of social indiscipline, deterioration of values, lack of social security etc.

Besides the potential stress that occurs outside the school, there are also those associated with the school itself. Teaching as a profession demands continuous growth, but teachers while discharging time for further studies, unable to utilize the training the salaries, lack of opportunity for reading training, less change for further promotion etc. are acting as source of stress on teachers.

Teaching as an occupation, present certain situation where in the teacher has to adjust to unhealthy school atmosphere, lack of recognition, for effective teaching. Teaching the subject is which he is not interested, lack of support for innovative approaches, lack of enthusiasm in staff meeting, monotonous working conditions, difference of opinions with head of the institution etc., are the situations acting as sources of stress.

Student behavior is also a major component in the teaching learning process. Continuous misbehavior or certain students, non-acceptance of teacher's authority indiscipline in the class, lack of interest on outsides. Threat from the students, lack of attention in the class, unable to estimate the student, lack of positive responses from the student etc., are some of the significant sources of stress on teachers. Thus, student as a group can be a significant source of teacher stress. Similarly lack of group cohesiveness in school, lack of social support and interpersonal conflicts create teacher stress.

So far, extra organizational, organizational and group stressors are discussed; teacher is the ultimate consumer of stress due to previously mentioned stressors. Thus individual dispositions such as role conflict and ambiguity at organizational and group levels, causes stress. Teachers have to play multiple roles and these often make conflicting expectation. In the present education system heavy expectation are there on teachers. Hence, teachers are supposed to undertake high magnitude of work.

Now teachers are experiencing stress as they are supposed to teach more periods a day without rest between periods, excess correction work, undertaking institutional work like censes lack of time for completing syllabus, conduct of co-curricular and extracurricular activities etc.

EFFECTS OF TEACHER STRESS

As job stress effect organizational performance, teacher stress impedes teacher performance in teaching. Infect it is assumed that mild stress can even enhance performance but high level of stress can create physical, Psychological and behavioral problems among teacher. There are several research studies, which observed that, a high level of stress accompanied by physical illness such as high blood pressures, ulcers and even cancer. Similarly high level of stress may be accompanied by psychological problems such as anger, anxiety, depression, nervousness, irritability, tension and boredom. Excessive stress may also result in behavioral problems such as sleeplessness, under eating or over eating, increased smoking and drinking and drug abuse. Many researches of teacher studies have established some strong correlates of teacher stress. From these researches, it has found that teacher stress related to job dissatisfaction (Rudd and Wiseman 1962; Krysacon and Suteliff 1979). Absenteeism, (Bridger 1980; Kaiser and Polezynsky 1982); greater intention to leave profession (Kryiacon and Suteliff 1979), Physical Distress (Coats and Thoresen, 1979) and teacher performance (Kkryiacon and Sutcliffe 1977-79, Pettegrew and Wolf 1982, Kaiser and Polezynsky 1982, Soloman 1960).

However, teaching competency has been recognized as important component of teaching learning process, relatively little effort is made to define the term. A peep in into the literature of teacher effectiveness as one finds many related terms such as teaching success; successful teacher, teaching efficiency, teacher performance, teacher competency etc.

"As one looks through heap of investigations in this field" Writes Barr (1961), "One finds various terms used to designate or describe the successful teacher. Frequently the word 'efficiency' is used one will not that the terms are sometimes applied to teacher as in teacher efficiency and sometimes in the teacher behavior as in the teaching efficiency.

Donald M. Medley (1982) States that the teacher competency as those of knowledge, abilities and beliefs on teacher processes and brings to the teaching situation. Teaching competency differs from teacher performance and teacher effectiveness in that it is a stable characteristic of the teacher that does not change appreciably when the teacher moves from one situation to another.

By this, it is evident that the knowledge of subject matter, teaching skills, beliefs and feelings of teacher may be considered as the components of teaching competent that a competent teacher is supposed to process.

Biddle (1964) advocates that "disagreement and ambiguity with respect to the description of teaching competence are to be expected and cannot entirely be avoided because competent teaching as undoubtedly a relative matter. Some investigators to refer to training process, properties of teachers, behavior exhibited by teacher and effects produced by teachers, have used the term competence. The same variable have been termed by other investigators as effectiveness, criteria of competency, ability in reach and a host of other terms-teacher success, teacher effectiveness, teacher efficiency, teacher performance, teacher competency etc., are used synonymously by investigators.

Researchers study teacher effectiveness in three component, presage, process and product. Here the presage component refers to thought processes, training aspect and personality factors of the teachers. The process component effects produced by teachers, the same variable have been termed by other investigators as effectiveness, criteria of competency, ability in reach and a host of other terms-teacher success, teacher effectiveness, teacher efficiency, teacher performance, teacher competency etc., are used synonymously by investigators.

Ryan (1960) States, "What constitutes effective teaching?" What are the distinguishing characteristics of competent teacher? are provocative and running questions unfortunately, no universally acceptable definite answers can be given to these complex queries-embarrassing as it may be for professional educators to recognize relatively little progress has been made."

Similarly, Biddle and Ellena accepted in 1966 that nobody knows what a competent teacher was. They said, "Probably no aspect of education has been discussed with greater frequency with as much deep concern or by more educators and citizens. The teacher effectiveness-How to define it, how to identify it, how to measure it, how to evaluate it, and how to detect and remove obstacles to its achievement-finding about the competence of teachers are inconclusive and peace meal and little is presently known for certain about teacher excellence.

Researchers study teacher effectiveness in three components; presage, process and product. Here the presage component refers to thought processes, training aspects and personality factors of the teachers. The process component to the teacher's action or classroom practices and the product component refer to the quality of the products i.e. students predicted.

Jangira (1979) states, "teacher's effectiveness has been considered into its three separate components for convenience of presentation. It should be taken that these components are watertight compartment. It also fallow that there are no clear-cut lines to distinguish one component from the other.

TEACHER COMPETENCY AND STRESS

The study is about teacher competency in relation to stress. Teacher competency, in general sense impedes, when teacher suffers from stress. In this chapter, a discussion is made about teacher competency, stress, and the development of this type of study in the world.

TEACHER COMPETENCY

One of the most difficult problems in educational research is that of recognizing teacher competency of discriminating between more and less effective teachers. The role of the classroom teacher in educational is central. The teacher is, after all, the point at contact between the educational system and the pupil. The impact of any educational programme or innovation on the pupil operates through the pupil's teacher. It is therefore quite accurate to say that a school's competence depends on the competence of its teachers. Maximizing teacher competence is a major goal of education.

"Teacher competency" refers to the behavior of a teacher while teaching a class (both inside and outside the classroom).Teacher performance differs from teacher competence. It is defined in terms of teacher behavior, of what the teacher does, teacher performance resembles teacher competence in that it is a product of interaction between certain teacher characteristics and the teaching situation-teacher performance is often used as a basis from which teacher competence can be inferred.

"Teacher competence" refers to the set of knowledge, abilities and beliefs a teacher process and bring to the teaching situation

Teacher competence differs from teacher performance and teacher effectiveness in that it is a stable characteristic of the teacher that does not change appreciably when the teacher moves from one situation to another. It resembles teacher performance in that it has also been proposed as a basis from which teacher effectiveness can be inferred.

Early Research: The first recorded study of teacher competence (Kratz, 1896), one of the earliest pieces of educational research of any kind to appear, set a design precedent that was to be followed for many years. A large group of elementary school pupils was asked to try to remember the best teacher each of them had ever encountered to write down what made that teacher different from others. Their descriptions were then collated and compared and from them was derived a list of characteristics that supposedly distinguished effective teachers from in effective ones. For the next half-century of so this kind of study was repeact6e again and again with groups chosen in various ways; sometime the task was performed by pupils currently attending schools sometimes by persons considered to be exports, educators, or teacher educators. Perhaps the most extensive and sophisticated example of this was the monumental common wealth teachers training study. (Charters of Waples 1929), which is used exhaustive and meticulous procedures to produce a number of lists of lengths. Typical of the characteristics listed were the following, which were the top six on a list of twenty-five.

1. Adaptability
2. Considerateness
3. Enthusiasm
4. Good judgment
5. Honesty
6. Magnetism

Pupil learning is a direct outcome of pupil learning experiences; learning is after all, something that pupils do not something teachers do. When a teacher “teacher’ what she or he really does is try to provide certain learning experiences for the pupils that all expected to bring about desired learning out-comes.

Whatever the nature of the teachers performance, different pupils will have different learning experiences and will make different amounts of gain. Since the unit of study in the process-product model of the class, not the pupil, learning outcomes must me measured in terms of class mean gain before they can be correlated with teacher performance, and variations in gain made by different pupils with the same class must be related as errors that attitude the correlations obtains.

DISSATISFACTION, STRESS AND BURNOUT

Do schools personnel have high moral and are they satisfied in their work setting? Newspaper headlines that emphasize teacher strikes, teacher burnout and stress on school employees suggest that many teachers are not satisfied. A number of studies conducted throughout the 1970s and into the 111980s indicate a gradual reduction in teacher satisfaction (for example, Fuller and Miskel (1972) found that about 89 percent of the teachers participating in this study were satisfied or very satisfied with their job. However, Bentzen, Williams and Heckman (1980), in an investigation conducted in the late 1970s, reported that slightly more than 75 percent of the teachers were satisfied with their jobs. In the later study, important difference in job satisfaction was discovered at the various levels of teaching, with elementary teachers expressing more satisfaction with their jobs than secondary teachers do. A nationwide poll of teachers conducted by the National Educational Association (NBA) in 1980 ("Teachers opinion poll: job satisfaction "1980) found that 35 percent of all public schoolteachers were dissatisfied with their current jobs. Two-fifths of the teacher said they would probably not become teachers if they had it to do all over again; one teacher in ten was planning to leave teaching as soon as possible, and another two teachers in ten were undecided about how long they would remain in teaching. These studies suggest a moderate trend in the direction of increasing dissatisfaction on the part of teachers-although a majority of school personnel continues to express satisfaction with this work.

SYMPTOMS AND CAUSES OF STRESS

Symptoms of teacher dissatisfaction and low morale vary. They include questioning and criticizing of school goals and polices, lack of enthusiasm for teaching rejection or lack of follow- up on administrative directives (Cook, 1979), absenteeism (Educational Research Service, 1980) and fragmentation, that is, a general feeling of being pulled in different directions (Klugman, Cartes &Israel, 1979). Some of these symptoms are also reported in a study by Staplenton, Craft and Frankiewicz (1979).

These researches found a positive relationship between teacher job satisfaction and teacher brink man ship, which they defined as teacher behavior that attempts to challenge the authority structure of the school while attempting to avoid its negative sanctions.

The causes of teacher stress and burnout are not easy to as certain nor are they easily distinguishable from the symptoms, although there is no shortage of suggested causes. With regard to teacher stress, quick and quick (1979) believe that four group of factors create work stress. 1) Role factors 2) job factors 3) physical factors and 4) interpersonal factors. They recommended a number of techniques for reducing the stress related by the various factors. The New York State United Teachers Organization that the most important factors contributing to stress is the effect of disruptive children, incompetent administrators are identifies as the second most important cause of stress ("Urban teachers report more stress", 1980).

In the New York stud, urban teachers reported more stress than did sub urban or rural teachers. Cichon and Koff, (1980) found in their research on Chicago teachers that the more important causes of teacher stress are problems of disruption and threats to the teacher's, physical professional and personal well being. In this connection, in NEA survey of its membership in 1980("teacher opinion poll attacks on teacher",1980)estimated that 1,13,000 of the country's 21,84,000 public school teachers were physically attacked by students during a recent twelve month period. Suggested causes of teaches burnout are usually believed to those associated with stress (block, 1978;weiskopt,1980).In a personal account of teacher burnout, Bardol (1979) has described several symptoms and perceived causes.

A number of investigations into the causes of teacher dissatisfaction have been conducted. An NEA survey ("teacher opinion poll; job satisfaction", 1980), found that a majority of teachers felt that the following factors, listed in order of frequency of identification had agentive of feet on their job satisfaction. 1. Public attitudes toward the school.2.treatment of education by the media.3.Student attitudes toward learning. 4. Salary and 5. Status of teachers in the community. In addition, 49 per cent of the teachers indicated that student behavior had negative effect upon their job satisfaction.

Ford (1979) believe that variables faculty workloads may be related to teacher dissatisfaction between class size and teacher satisfaction is investigated (Glass, et al., 1979,Pages and price (1980)discovered in their study of 130 teachers that the factors contributing most to job dissatisfaction are in order of important.1.lack of planning time. 2. Tedious paper and clerical work 3.On out of tough and autocratic administration.4. Disruptive and unmotivated student's 5.Non teaching activities, such as faculty meeting and "time wasting" workshop 6.Uncooperative parents 7.Lack of autonomy to prescribe curriculum 8.Feeling of failure and 9.Low occupational prestige.

Thus, a brief discussion and outline is presented in the chapter about matters relating to teacher competency and stress. Thus, this kind of analysis gave the investigator. Some clues on the subject on the hand.

2

Reviev of the Related Literature

The investigator reviewed the available related literature pertaining to teacher stress and teaching competency for the present study and presented as follows.

1. Studies related to Teacher stress.
2. Studies related to Teaching competency.

MOHOLICK'S (1969), MASTACH AND JACKSONS (1980)

STUDIES RELATED TO TEACHER STRESS

A study of meaning in life, Stress and Burnout in Teachers of Secondary Schools in Calcutta.

OBJECTS OF THE STUDY

1. To study if teachers varied in the degree of overall meaning in life and if they showed a trend low or high meaning.
2. To identify important sources of meaning in the personal and professional life of teachers and to investigate if teachers varied in the degree of meaning derived from these sources.

3. To find out the relationship, if any among the different measures of meaning in life.
4. To identify the main sources of stress in teaching and to investigate if teachers varied in the extent of experienced stress.
5. To study if teachers varied in the extent of perceived.
6. To study the relationship between stress and burnout meaning

The tools used for data collection were Moholick's (1969) purpose in life Test, Mastach and Jackson (1981) inventory for study of burnout and a scale and interview schedules prepared by the investigator for measurement of stress and other background variables. The sample comprised 345 teachers from 15 secondary schools and an in service teachers Population of three teacher training institutions in Calcutta. Survey and case study techniques were followed in the conduct of the study. Descriptive and non-parametric statistical techniques were used for analysis of data.

FINDINGS THE STUDY

1. Meaningfulness of life of the teachers was quite high according to their own perception.
2. Meaning in professional life was derived primarily from psychic reward obtained from task related outcomes and relationship with the student.
3. All the measures of meaning in life namely self reported meaning in life, source of meaning in life and sources of meaning in teaching had a political relationship with meaning of life.
4. The relationship between stress studied through test and stress reported by teachers was highly significant.
5. Age difference was significant with regard to stress of teachers.
6. The sample teachers had a lower degree of burnout.
7. Sex difference was significant on the burnout variable.

8. Stress was positively related to burnout with regard to emotional exhaustion and depersonalization.
9. There was negative relationship between meaning in life and stress variables measured by tests as well as self – reporting items.
10. A comparatively low level of meaning in life was identified among the sample teachers.

STUDIES RELATED TO TEACHING COMPETENCY

L.S.VERNE.M.R.,L.V.C.U.1985

A STUDY OF SOME OF THE PERSONALITY COMPONENT OF CREATIVE STUDENT TEACHERS IN RELATION TO THEIR COMPETENCE TOWARDS TEACHING.

The study was designed to compare high, medium and low creative student teachers on three dimensions of creativity and total creativity in terms of certain personality components sex, Teaching competence and achievement levels.

The sample consisted of 210 B.Ed., students randomly select from our educational instructions in Lucknow. Data regarding creative were collected with the help of tolerance Test of creative thinking. For assessment personality characteristics, the multivariate personality inventory and 16PF were administered to the student teachers. A teacher effectiveness scale was administered to get an idea about their effectiveness as teachers and division scored by them in practice teaching was taken as the criterion of their performance as teachers. Main findings of the study:

(1) The F ratio for the effect of fluency was significant for dominance-reserved vs. outgoing, humble vs. assertive and tough-minded vs. tender minded.

(2) The F ratio for the main effects of flexibility were significant for ego ideal, dominance, sober vs. happy-go-luck and group-dependent vs. self-sufficient.

(3) The F ratio for the effect of originality was significant for self-confidence humble vs. assertive and sober vs. happy-go-lucky.

(4) The F ratio for the effect of total creativity were significant for empathy, self confidence, reserved vs. outgoing sober vs. happy-go-lucky and taught minded vs. tender minded.

(5) The F ratio for the interaction of sex and total creativity was significant for neuroticism, self confidence and reserved vs. outgoing

(6) Personality factors distinguishing the low total creativity group from the medium total creativity group were self-confidence, thought minded vs. tender minded and sober vs. happy-go-luck.

NATARAJAN.S. MADRAS-U

A competency based Program in Teacher Education Curriculum:

The major objectives of these investigations were;

1. To study the relative efficiency of competency based teacher education in the pre-service education program of secondary school teachers.
2. To identify factors influencing competency achievement such as social status, economic status and level of education and.
3. To find out the relationship between an individual's self-esteem and competency achievement.

MAJOR FINDINGS OF THE STUDY

1. Competency-based instruction proved suitable for teaching selected units in institutions, planning and administration.
2. The seminar method seemed to be an effective method as it compared favourable with the competency-based approach.
3. The lecture method was effective as a group method.
4. Directed self-study did not compare well with other methods.
5. There was a significant relation between self-esteem and acquisition of competencies.

6. Attitude towards teaching methods had a favorable correlation with acquisition of competencies.
7. The study proved that teacher education programme could be made more effective through a competency-based approach.

BHALWANKARA.G.

SNDT COLLEGE OF EDUCATION-PUNE-1984

SIE MAHARASTRA FINANCED

A Study of Reliability and Validity of the Process-Process Appraising Scale of Teacher of Effectiveness.

THE MAJOR OBJECTIVES OF THE STUDY:

1. To determine the reliability of the process-process appraising scale of teacher.
2. To determine criterion related to and the content validity of the PASTE.
3. To determine the relationship between various component scores of PASTE teacher effectiveness scores on PASTE.
4. To study the effect of increase or decrease in number of components of PASTE on reliability and
5. To determine the relationship between presage variables and teacher effectiveness scores of student teacher.

THE MAJOR FINDINGS OF THE STUDY

1. The reliability of PASTE by four-way analysis of variance was 0.72; the reliability of PASTE was quite satisfactory.
2. PASTE had satisfactory content and criterion related validity.
3. All the components correlated positively with the total teacher 3effectiveness score some skills were significant related to total teacher effectiveness.

SINGH.R.S.,GOR.-1987

A STUDY OF TEACHER'S EFFECTIVENESS AND ITS CORRELATES AT HIGHER SECONDARY STAGE IN EASTERN.

MAJOR OBJECTIVES OF THE STUDY

1. To compare teacher effectiveness of Male and Female teachers of Urban and Rural area.
2. To compare their intelligence, socio-economic status, attitude towards teaching profession and adjustment.
3. To find out the relationship between teacher effectiveness and
4. To determine the combined effect of the correlates on teacher effectiveness.

The sample comprised 330 teachers of Urban and Rural areas from 22 intermediate colleges of Varanasi, Gorekhpur and Jaunpur districts. The tools used were teacher attitude inventory. Teacher adjustment inventory, SES Scale, Samoohik, Mansik Yogyata, Prakash (1/61) and teaching effectiveness rating scale.

THE MAJOR FINDINGS

1. No significant difference in the mean scores of male and female teachers in their effectiveness was observed.
2. The difference in the mean intelligence scores of male and female teachers was not significant.
3. It was revealed that the rural female teachers had secured comparatively better scores than the rural male teachers in teacher effectiveness.
4. The difference in the mean scores of urban male and female teachers was found to be non-significant on the SES scale.
5. There was no-significant difference in the mean scores of male and female teachers belonging to rural and urban area in their attitude towards teaching.
6. There was no-significant difference in the mean scores of adjustment of male and female teachers.
7. The scores of male and female teachers in teaching effectiveness appeared to be correlated significantly with only two variables-intelligence and attitudes towards the teaching profession.

8. A low relationship between intelligence and socio-economic status was observed. It was however not significant.
9. The teacher effectiveness scores of rural male and female teachers appeared to significantly relate with intelligence, socio-economic status and adjustment.
10. Intelligence showed a moderate and significant relationship with socio-economic status and adjustment of the urban teachers irrespective of sex.

SUSHILA SINGHAL; Stress in Education Indian Experience, Rawat publication, New Delhi, 2004, pp. 294-334.

THE MAJOR FINDINGS

The personal profiles of teachers are not much important, as most of them show mild to moderate levels of stress and burnout, yet the older and those having higher educational qualifications seem to be more stress prone. Those having higher socio-economic status are more involved with students and feel more responsible, but become less idealistic over the tears. In the regular as well as in special schools, teachers experience different levels of stress. So do the males and females, and the more vs. less experienced teachers. The negative perceptions of work-setting can induce negative feelings in teachers resulting in subsequent stress and burnout. Female teachers tend to perceive the work-setting as more positive than males. The special schoolteachers rate their work load higher; their contacts with students more frequent and intense feel more socially isolated and have more role conflicts. More experienced teachers have fewer interpersonal interactions, yet lower social isolation and fewer conflicts in regular as well as special schools. The work-setting of regular schools emerges as the necessary condition, and the stress as the sufficient condition for the onset of burnout. All teachers experience moderate levels of burnout, indicating something more can activate it to be a matter of concern. Males and females both experience it evenly. Teachers in the middle range of experience are more susceptible to stress and burnout than those with a few years or long experience. The finding of work-setting dimensions explaining a higher percent of variance in burnout is interesting to indicate that neither stress is independent of work context, nor all stress gets converted into burnout. Absence of adequate interpersonal interactions and positive feedback, bureaucratic hindrances, greater role conflicts, and difficult and problematic students are good predictors of burnout. Lack of proper training is a good predictor of burnout in special school teachers. The work overload, inadequate orientation few interpersonal interactions, and more role conflicts are associated with greater self-interest. Higher social isolation leads to reduced work goals. Those facing more role conflicts tend to become emotionally detached. The improvements in work-setting need to be initiated to suit the needs of the teachers so that they can efficaciously deliver instruction to their pupils and derive satisfaction from their performance.

3

Methods of Investigation

The present study is titled "A study of the Factors Influencing Teachers Stress among the School Teachers in Chittoor".

NEED FOR THE STUDY

Accomplishment of educational goals and the objectives of teaching is possible only with teachers those who are competent in teaching and free from any type of stress. Teacher stress directly or indirectly influences the competency of teachers in teaching. So the teacher who is subjected to stress may not be possible to teach properly which in term competency in teaching.

Theoretically, the teacher stress may be heard to perform teaching in a competent way. But in practice how far teacher stress is influencing on teaching competency and to what extent teacher stress and teaching competency are related-are the questions waiting for answer. Hence, this study has taken up to find out how teacher stress and teaching competency are inter-related to each other in the context of high school education.

Design is the heart of research. The following aspects have been discussed in detail, which are concerned with the design of the present study. The present chapter is set apart for making a brief discussion of the objectives of the study, the research procedure includes the operational definitions of the different terms used the various hypotheses that were framed for verification in the present study and the rationale of these hypotheses. The selection of sample includes the sampling techniques used, the reasons for selection of a particular sampling technique and the selection of the sample according to different variables. The selection of suitable tool for collection of data and the procedure followed in administering the tool to collect the data required for the present study.

PROBLEM OF THE SUDY

In the view of the previous chapter, the investigator titled the problem in the following manner. "A study of factors Influencing Teacher's Stress among the School Teachers in Chittoor"

OBJECTIVES OF THE STUDY

1. To test the teacher stress and teaching competency scales to be use by the teacher himself.
2. To find out the relationship between teacher stress and teaching competency.
3. To find out the effect of demographical variables in respect of teacher stress.
4. To find out the effect of demographical variables in respect of teaching competency.

ITEM ANALYSIS

For the purpose of determining the degree to which each item is effective in discriminating between high and low teaching competency and item analysis of the data obtained from above sample is undertaken by taking two extreme groups (High and Low) All the fifty two responses of the 200 subjects are scored and scores are arranged in an order from highest score to lowest score. Then the upper 27 per cent of the responses and lower 27per cent of the responses are taken into consideration for measuring significance of difference of means to know the item validity. A.M.S. and S.D.S for the 46 items of upper half and lower half are calculated for all the 46 items between upper and lower half using the following formula.

If the value of the critical ratio 0 the item is greater than 1. 96 (significant at 0.05 level of significant). Then the item is found valid and accepted. If the value of critical ratio of item is less than 1.96 then the item is found invalid and rejected.

RE-TESTING OF TEACHER STRESS SCALE

In the present study, the investigator adopted the Rama's teacher stress self-rating five-point scale developed and standardized by. Dr. Krishnan Raju (1994) because it is more appropriate to measure the teacher stress related to the areas of 1.Professional growth, 2. Work load 3). Occupational Hazards 4).Student behavior 5). Family 6), Societal

The present investigator re-tested this scale on a tryout sample of 200teachers to minimize the error in the tool. There are 46 items under six different areas of teacher stress scale of Dr. Krishnan Raju. The distribution or 52 items is as fallows. Items under professional growth area of teacher stress are 8 i.e., from 1to 8.

1. Items under workload area of teacher stress are 9 i.e., from 9 to 17.
2. Items under occupational Hazards area are of teacher stress are 9 i.e., 18 to26.
3. Items under student behavior area of teacher stress are 9 i.e., 27 to 35.
4. Items under family area of teacher stress are 8 i.e., 36 to43.
5. Items under society area of teacher stress are 3 i.e., 3.

ADMINISRRATION

This tool I administered to a try out samples of 200 teachers of Chittoor. Instructions to the teachers are given on the title page of the scale. Care is taken to reduce bias in rating. This is done by clearly stating the purpose of study.

Table-1

Showing the number of items and percentage of items in teachers stress.

	Professional Growtho	Work Load	Occupational Hazards	Student Behavior	Family	Societal	Total
No.of Queo	8	9	9	9	8	3	**46**
%	16.9	15.2	16.9	.9	16.9	16.9	**99.7**

SCORING

The responses are scored according to the key. The scoring procedure, which was followed in the teacher competency scale, is followed to this teacher stress also. Total number of items is 46. The maximum is 230 and the minimum possible score is 46 the high score indicates high teacher stress; the low score indicates low teacher stress.

ITEM ANALYSIS

For the purpose of determining the degree to which each item is effective in discriminating high, low stress of teacher an item analysis of the data obtained from the above sample is under taken by taking two extreme groups (High and low) All the 46 responses of the 200subjects are scored and total scores are arranged in an order from highest score to lowest score. Then the upper 27per cent of the total response and lower 27 per cent of total responses are taken into consideration. For measuring significance of the items retained after item analysis for the final student in teacher difference of means to know item validity A.M.S and SDS for all the 46 items of the upper half and lower half are calculated. Critical ratio is then calculated for all the items between upper and lower halves. If the value of critical for ratio of the items is greater than 1.96 (significant at 0.05 level of significance). Then the item is found valid and accepted. If the value of the critical ratio of the item is less than 1.96 then the item is found as invalid and rejected.

COLLECTION OF DATA

After retesting the two tools of the study, fresh and final scales are prepared for the final study with personal data pose. There two standardized tools of the resent study are administered to 200teacher of different schools in Chittioor of A.P. for collecting the data the investigator visited each school and administered the scales to the teachers personally. They are advised to put their name, sex, qualification, designation, experience etc. against the place provided in the personal data sheet of each scale.

Instructions are given in the first page of each scale. The investigator requested the teacher to fallow the instruction while responding the tools. Most of the teachers filled the tools on the spot and returned to the investigator. These two tools collected and scored according to the scoring procedure explained in the development and standardization of tools.

SAMPLE

The sample selected for the present investigation consist 200 teachers of different Schools in Chittoor of A.P. The age of the teachers up to 35 and above 35 years, both male and female teachers are found in the sample. Teachers having 2 slabs experience i.e. above15 years, below 15 years are found in the sample. Teachers of two cadres of P.G. and graduate teachers. Another sample Government teacher. Thus, it is found to be a satisfactory sample and the sample is believed to be adequate to test the hypothesis.

The sample distribution of the study is shown in below

AGE IN YEARS	**ABOVE 35** 121	**BELOW 35○** 79
SEX	**MALE** 88	**FEMALE○** 112
GENERAL QUALIFICATION	**GRADUATES** 100	**P.G** 100

TEACHIN GEXPERIENCE	**ABOVE 35** 84	**BELOW 35**○ 116
MANAGEMENT	**GOVT.** 99	**PRIVATE**○ 101

ANALYSIS OF DATA

The following statistical techniques are used to analyze the data.

Mean and standard deviations of all the distributions are calculated.

To find out the relationship between teaching competency and Teacher stress "r" values are computed.

Co-efficiency of co-relation for the entire dimension was also calculated.

Critical ratios are calculated for testing the subsidiary hypothesis.

HYPOTHESES OF THE STUDY

1. There is no significant difference between Above 35 years age of teachers and Below 35 years age of teacher towards teacher stress.
2. There is no significant difference between Male and Female teachers towards teacher stress.
3. There is no significant difference between Graduate teachers and post Graduate Teachers towards teacher stress.
4. There is no significant difference between Above 15 tears, and Below 15 years teaching experience towards teacher stress.
5. There is no significant difference between Government School Teachers and Private school Teachers towards teacher stress.
6. There is no significant difference between Male and Female Teachers towards teacher stress in Professional growth.
7. There is no significant difference between Male and Female Teachers towards teacher stress in Work Load.

8. There is no significant difference between Male and Female Teachers towards teacher stress in Occupational Hazards.
9. There is no significant difference between Male and Female Teachers towards teacher stress in Student Behavior.
10. There is no significant difference between Male and Female Teachers towards teacher stress in Family.
11. There is no significant difference between Graduate teachers and Post Graduate Teachers towards teacher stress in Professional Growth
12. There is no significant difference between Graduate teachers and Post Graduate Teachers towards teacher stress in Work Load
13. There is no significant difference between Graduate teachers and Post Graduate Teachers towards teacher stress in Occupational Hazards.
14. There is no significant difference between Graduate teachers and Post Graduate Teachers towards teacher stress in Student Behavior
15. There is no significant difference between Graduate teachers and Post Graduate Teachers towards teacher stress in Family.

LIMITATIONS OF THE STUDY

1. The study is limited to only teachers of different primary and secondary schools in Chittoor of A.P.
2. Of the three criteria of teaching competency, only two criteria i.e. presage and process are covered in this study.
3. To measure the teaching competency and teacher stress teacher self –rating scales are used in this study.
4. Of many dimensions of teaching competency, planning presentation, closing evaluation, and managerial dimensions are considered in this study.
5. Of many dimensions of teacher stress professional growth, work load, Occupational hazards, Students behavior, family and societal dimensions are considered in this study

PROCEDURE

In order to test the Hypothesis the investigator planned and executed in three steps

(1) Measurement of teacher stress with the help of standardized teacher stress,

(2) Measurement of teaching competency with the help of Rama's teaching competency scale.

(3) Using appropriate statistical procedures to find out relationship between teacher stress and teaching competency.

RE-TESTING OF RAMA'S TEACHER STRESS SCALE

In the present study, the investigator adopted the Rama's teacher stress self rating five point scale developed and standardized by Prof. R. Rama (2004) because it is more appropriate to measure the teacher stress related to the areas of

1. Professional Growth 2. Workload 3. Occupational Hazards 4. Student Behavior 5. Family 6. Societal.

   - There are 46 items under 6 different areas of teacher stress scale of Prof. R. Rama.
   - Items under professional growth area of teacher stress are 8 i.e., from 1to 8.
   - Items under Work Load area of teacher stress are 9 i.e., from 9 to 17.
   - Items under Occupational Hazards area of teacher stress are 9 i.e., from18 to 26.
   - Items under Student Behavior area of teacher stress are 9 i.e., from 27 to 35.
   - Items under Family area of teacher stress are 8 i.e., from 36 to 43.
   - Items under Societal area of teacher stress are 3 i.e., from 44 to 46.

Table - 2

Variable wise distribution of the Sample

Variable	Categories	Size	Grand Total
Sex	Male	85	200
	Female	115	
Age	Above 35	129	200
	Below 35	71	
Qualification	Graduate	92	200
	Post-Graduate	108	
Management	Government	99	200
	Private	101	
TeachingExperience	Above 15	92	200
	Below 15	108	

SELECTION OF THE TOOL

A research tool plays a major role in any worthwhile research as it is the sole factor is determining the sound data and in arriving at perfect conclusions about the problem or study on hand, which ultimately, helps in providing suitable remedial measures to the problem concerned.

The progress of making depends upon well-conducted research programme. Well conducted research programmes postulate sufficient, reliable and valid facts such facts are obtained through a systematic procedure, which involves various devices. Each rehear tool is appropriate in a given situation to accomplish a particular purpose. It may be stressed that these tools may be used in combination. They supplement the work of each other.

John Best observes, “Like the tools in the carpenter box, each research tool is appropriate in a given situation to accomplish a particular purpose”. Each data gathering –device has both merits and Hazards of limitations.

Different tools are used to collect various kinds of information for different purposes. The investigator should familiarize themselves with nature, merits and limitations of these tools and should attempt to learn how to construct and use them effectively.

The following are some of the tools generally employed for the purpose of research.

(a) Inquiry forms:

1. Questionnaire
2. Schedule
3. Check-list
4. Rating scale
5. Score card
6. Attitude scale

(b) Observation

(c) Interview

(d) Sociometry

(e) Psychological tests:

1. Achivement test
2. Aptitude test
3. Intelligence test
4. Interest Inventory
5. Personality measures

Inequity forms are class of data gathering devices which make use of properly prepared Performa or forms for enquiring into and securing information about certain phenomena under study. Out of number of such inequity forms, perhaps the most used and the most abused of tools is the questionnaire.

Keeping in view the desirability and suitability for the collection of the data, the investigator adapted the questionnaire in case of the present investigation.

ADMINISTRATION OF THE TOOL

The investigator personally went to each institution and has taken permission from the respective head of the institutions and personally administered to 200 teachers in the various schools. The investigator first explained to the teachers about the importance of the investigation and attitude of teachers towards teacher stress in relation to teaching competency in school teachers. As stated earlier, the present investigation is intended to the attitudes of schoolteachers.

ANALISIS OF THE DATA

The following statistical techniques are followed to analyze of the data.

1. Mean and Standard Deviation of all the distributions are calculated.
2. To find out the relationship between teacher stress and teaching competency 'r' values are computed. The analyze and interpretation of the present data is presented in proceeding Chapter

SCORING PROCEDURE

The responses are scored in stress according to key, for all the items scores from five to one for the five responses i.e. N. S. (No stress), Mi. S (Mild stress), Mo. S (Moderate Stress), M. S.(More Stress), S. S. (Sevier Stress) total No. of items 46 in teacher stress scale.

Table-3:
The weightage given to responses

KIND OF RESPONSES	MARKS○
No Stress (N.S)	5
Mild Stress (Mi. S.)	4
Moderate Stress (Mo. S.)	3
More Stress (M. S.)	2
Sevier Stress (S. S.)	1

STITISTICAL TECHNIQUES USED

The above-mentioned hypotheses, which were framed keeping the variables like age, sex, teaching experience, medium of teaching, Qualification Type of management were taken into consideration. The collected data analyzed and the results are interpreted and statistical aspects like means, standard deviation and critical ratios are taken as the statistical techniques to study and analyze the variables. Co-efficient of co-relation with the help of scatter diagram was made use of to study the reliability of the test scores. The technique of the significance of the difference between means is used. Here technique only large samples in different categories considered for comparison so that use was made only of the formula for large samples. It was further assumed that the means were uncorrelated.

Where

A.M =Arithmetic mean

A.A.M = Assumed arithmetic mean

S.D = Standard deviation

C.R = Critical Ratio

1,2 = Standard deviation of two samples

M1, m2 = Means of the two samples

N1,N2 = The size of the two sample

4

Analysis and Interpretation of the Data

INTRODUCTION

Data analysis is the heart of any social science research. Using questionnaire or any inventory the researcher collects the information. Until and unless, it is proposed through statistical treatment, it serves no purpose. The researcher using the standardized procedure that tool so constructed collected data from various variables. The he collected information is given numerical scoring and scores are tabulated. The mean, median, mode, quartile deviation, standard deviation, kurtosis etc. are also obtained. Basing on the responses of the individuals the the researcher tabulated the item of the tool according to their scoring order presented findings and calculations. Finally, the researcher presented suggestions for the teacher stress in relation to teaching competency scope for further research.

ANALYSIS

The analysis and interpretation of data involves the objectives material in the processions of the research and his subjective and desires to derive from the data, the inherent meaning in their relation to the problem. To avoid making conclusions are interpretations from insufficient are invalid data, the final analysis must be anticipated in detailed when plans are being made for collecting information.

J. C. Agarwal, has explained thus:"However values, reliable and adequate the data may be, it does not serve any worthwhile purpose unless it is carefully edited. Systematically analyzed intelligently interpreted and rationally concluded".

Analysis of data means studying the tabulated material in order to determine inherent facts of meaning. It involves breaking down existing complex factors into smaller parts and putting the together in new arrangements for purposes interpretation.

THE FOLLOWING ARE THE METHODS MOST COMMONLY USED IN STATISTICAL ANALYSIS

1. Calculating frequency distribution (usually in percentage) of items under study.
2. Testing the data for morality of distribution-Skewness and Kurtosis.
3. Calculating methods of central tendency –Mean, Median, Mode and establishing norms.
4. Calculating percentile and percentile ranks.
5. Calculating measures of dispersion –Standard deviation, Mean deviation, Quartile deviation and Range.
6. Calculating measures of relationship-Coefficient of correlation reliability and validity.
7. Graphical representation of data –Frequency Polygon curve, Hectograph, Cumulative frequency, Polygon and Ogive etc.

In the process of analysis of the data, the investigators usually make used of us many of the above simply statistical devises as necessary for purpose of their study. There are some other complicated devices of statistical analysis which researches use in particular experimental or complex casual comparative studies investigation.

INTERPRETATION

"The process of interpretation is essentially one of the stating what the results (findings) show, what do they means What is their significance What is the answer to original problem. Interpretation is thus by no means a much of process. Its uses of scientific examination of the results of one's analysis in the light of all the limitations of the data gathering, Interpretation means the application of deductive and inductive logic to the research process.

Interpretation is the most important step in the total procedure of research, it is purely subjective and many errors are made at their stage.

An adequate knowledge not only of techniques of research, but also of one's field of study and a capacity to do carefully and critical thinking are very essential to safe guard against misinterpretation of facts collected.

The analysis and interpretation of the data represent the application of deductive and inductive logic to the research process. Interpretation calls for a critical examination of the result of one's analysis in the light of all the limitation of the data gathering and his subjective attitude to avoid subjectively, one must be critical on one's own thinking.

Good, Barr and Scats the following characteristics of good generalizations.

1. Education generalization should be conceivable and in agreement with facts.
2. They should not conflict with the known laws of nature of previously established generalization.
3. They should be stated in the simplest possible terms.
4. They should be amenable to deductive reasoning.

In this part the result of present study are analyzed and interpreted. The results are presented and all the hypotheses are tested and verified in the present study, the results are analyzed and presented in three parts.

1. The first part deals with related to significant relationship between the teacher stress and teaching competency.

2. The second part deals with testing the hypotheses pertaining to teacher stress.
3. The third part deals with testing the hypotheses pertaining to teaching competency.

TESTING OF HYPOTHESES - 1

There is no significant difference between above 35 years age of teachers and blow 35 years age of teachers towards teachers stress. To test the validity of the above hypothesis, the following calculations are made. Table showing the significant difference between above 35 years age of teachers and below 35 years age of teacher in respect of teachers stress.

TABLE - 4

AGE	N	MEAN	SD	't' VALUE
1.00	129	161.66	35.70	0.56
2.00	71	158.87	29.49	@

From the above table the calculated 't' value is 0.56 found to be less than the table value (1.96) at 0.05 level. Hence, the hypothesis-1 is accepted. Hence, there is no significance difference between above 35 years age of teachers and below 35 years age of teachers towards teacher stress.

TESTING OF HYPOTHESES - 2

There is no significant difference between male and female teachers towards teacher stress. To test the validity of the above hypothesis, the following calculations are made. The table showing the significant differences between male and female teachers in respect of teacher stress.

TABLE - 5

SEX	N	MEAN	SD	't' VALUE
1.00	85	28.41	6.02	1.54
2.00	115	29.78	6.33	@

From the above table the calculated 't' value is 1.54 found to be less than the table value (1.96) at 0.05 level. Hence, the hypothesis-2 is accepted. Hence, there is no significance difference between male and female teacher towards teacher stress.

TESTING OF HYPOTHESES - 3

There is no significant difference between graduate teachers and post-graduate teachers towards teacher stress. To test the validity of the above hypothesis, the following calculations are made. The table showing the significant differences between graduate teachers and post-graduate teachers in respect of teacher stress.

TABLE - 6

EDUCATIONAL QUALIFICATION	N	MEAN	SD	't' VALUE
1.00	92	164.22	37.00	1.386
2.00	108	157.63	30.20	@

From the above table the calculated 't' value is 1.386 found to be greater than the table value (1.96) at 0.05 level. Hence, the hypothesis-3 is accepted. Hence, there no is significance difference between graduate teacher and post-graduate teachers towards teacher stress.

TESTING OF HYPOTHESES - 4

There is no significant difference between above 15 years, and below 15 years teaching experience towards teacher stress. To test the validity of the above hypothesis, the following calculations

TABLE - 7

TEACHING EXPERIENCE	N	MEAN	SD	't' VALUE
1.00	92	159.78	36.488	0.344
2.00	108	161.42	31.044	@

are made. The table showing the significant differences between teaching experience of above 15 years and below 15 years towards in respect of teacher stress.

From the above table the calculated 't' value is 0.344 found to be greater than the table value (1.96) at 0.05 level. Hence, the hypothesis-4 is accepted. Hence, there is no significance difference between experience of above 15 years and below 15 years towards teacher stress.

TESTING OF HYPOTHESES - 5

There is no significant difference between govt. school teachers and private school teachers towards teacher stress. To test the validity of the above hypothesis, the following calculations are made. The table showing the significant differences between govt. school teachers and private school teachers towards in respect of teacher stress.

TABLE - 8

TYPE OF MANAGEMENT	N	MEAN	SD	't' VALUE
1.00	91	161.67	32.47	0.419
2.00	108	159.68	34.76	@

From the above table the calculated 't' value is 0.419 found to be greater than the table value (1.96) at 0.05 level. Hence, the hypothesis-5 is accepted. Hence, there is no significance difference between govt. school teachers and private school teachers towards teacher stress.

TESTING OF HYPOTHESES - 6

There is no significant difference between male and female teachers towards teacher stress in professional growth. To test the validity of the above hypothesis, the following calculations are made. The table showing the significant differences between male and female teachers in respect of teacher stress in professional growth.

TABLE - 9

SEX	N	MEAN	SD	't' VALUE
1.00	85	28.41	6.02	01.544
2.00	115	29.78	6.33	@

From the above table the calculated 't' value is 01.544 found to be less than the table value (1.96) at 0.05 level. Hence, the hypothesis-6 is accepted. Hence, there is no significance difference between male and female teacher towards teacher stress in professional growth.

TESTING OF HYPOTHESES - 7

There is no significant difference between male and female teachers towards teacher stress in work load. To test the validity of the above hypothesis, the following calculations are made. The table showing the significant differences between male and female teachers in respect of teacher stress in work load.

TABLE - 10

SEX	N	MEAN	SD	't' VALUE
1.00	85	30.20	8.22	0.939
2.00	115	31.32	8.44	@

From the above table the calculated't' value is -.939 found to be greater than the table value (1.96) at 0.05 level. Hence, the hypothesis-7 is accepted. Hence, there is no significance difference between male and female teacher towards teacher stress in workload.

TESTING OF HYPOTHESES - 8

There is no significant difference between male and female teachers towards teacher stress in occupational hazards. To test the validity of the above hypothesis, the following calculations are made. The table showing the significant differences between male and female teachers in respect of teacher stress in occupational hazards.

TABLE - 11

SEX	N	MEAN	SD	't' VALUE
1.00	85	31.44	7.34	0.685
2.00	115	32.20	7.91	@

From the above table the calculated 't' value is 0.685 found to be greater than the table value (1.96) at 0.05 level. Hence, the hypothesis-8 is accepted. Hence, there is no significance difference between male and female teacher towards teacher stress in occupational hazards.

TESTING OF HYPOTHESES - 9

There is no significant difference between male and female teachers towards teacher stress in student behaviour. To test the validity of the above hypothesis, the following calculations are made. The table showing the significant differences between male and female teachers in respect of teacher stress in student behaviour.

TABLE - 12

SEX	N	MEAN	SD	't' VALUE
1.00	85	30.87	8.51	1.386
2.00	115	29.26	7.81	@

From the above table the calculated 't' value is 1.386 found to be greater than the table value (1.96) at 0.05 level. Hence, the hypothesis-9 is accepted. Hence, there is no significance difference between male and female teacher towards teacher stress in student behaviour.

TESTING OF HYPOTHESES - 10

There is no significant difference between male and female teachers towards teacher stress in family. To test the validity of the above hypothesis, the following calculations are made. The table showing the significant differences between male and female teachers in respect of teacher stress in family.

TABLE - 13

SEX	N	MEAN	SD	't' VALUE
1.00	85	28.01	7.266	1.305
2.00	115	29.417	7.72	@

From the above table the calculated 't' value is 1.305 found to be greater than the table value (1.96) at 0.05 level. Hence, the hypothesis-10 is accepted. Hence, there is no significance difference between male and female teacher towards teacher stress in family.

TESTING OF HYPOTHESES - 11

There is no significant difference between graduate teachers and post-graduate teachers towards stress in professional growth. To test the validity of the above hypothesis, the following calculations are made. The table showing the significant differences between graduate teachers and post-graduate teachers in respect of teacher stress in professional growth.

TABLE - 14

EDUCATIONAL QUALIFICATION	N	MEAN	SD	't' VALUE
1.00	92	29.81	6.70	1.291
2.00	108	28.67	5.77	@

From the above table the calculated 't' value is 1.291 found to be greater than the table value (1.96) at 0.05 level. Hence, the hypothesis-11 is accepted. Hence, there is no significance difference between graduate teacher and post-graduate teachers towards teacher stress in professional growth.

TESTING OF HYPOTHESES - 12

There is no significant difference between graduate teachers and post-graduate teachers towards stress in workload. To test the validity of the above hypothesis, the following calculations are made. The table showing the significant differences between graduate teachers and post-graduate teachers in respect of teacher stress in workload.

TABLE - 15

EDUCATIONAL QUALIFICATION	N	MEAN	SD	't' VALUE
1.00	92	32.4348	8.3827	2.518
2.00	108	29.4907	8.1166	*

From the above table the calculated 't' value is 2.518 found to be less than the table value (1.96) at 0.05 level. Hence, the hypothesis-12 is rejected. Hence, there is significance difference between graduate teacher and post-graduate teachers towards teacher stress in workload.

TESTING OF HYPOTHESES - 13

There is no significant difference between graduate teachers and post-graduate teachers towards stress in occupational hazards. To test the validity of the above hypothesis, the following calculations are made. The table showing the significant differences between graduate teachers and post-graduate teachers in respect of teacher stress in occupational hazards.

TABLE - 16

EDUCATIONAL QUALIFICATION	N	MEAN	SD	't' VALUE
1.00	92	32.3696	8.2405	0.832
2.00	108	31.4630	7.1662	@

From the above table the calculated 't' value is 0.832 found to be greater than the table value (1.96) at 0.05 level. Hence, the hypothesis-13 is accepted. Hence, there is no significance difference between graduate teacher and post-graduate teachers towards teacher stress in occupational hazards.

TESTING OF HYPOTHESES - 14

There is no significant difference between graduate teachers and post-graduate teachers towards stress in student behaviour. To test the validity of the above hypothesis, the following calculations are made. The table showing the significant differences between graduate teachers and post-graduate teachers in respect of teacher stress in student behaviour.

TABLE - 17

EDUCATIONAL QUALIFICATION	N	MEAN	SD	't' VALUE
1.00	92	30.0109	8.7549	0.105
2.00	108	29.8889	7.6162	@

From the above table the calculated 't' value is 0.105 found to be greater than the table value (1.96) at 0.05 level. Hence, the hypothesis-14 is accepted. Hence, there is no significance difference between graduate teacher and post-graduate teachers towards teacher stress in student behaviour.

TESTING OF HYPOTHESES - 15

There is no significant difference between graduate teachers and post-graduate teachers towards stress in family. To test the validity of the above hypothesis, the following calculations are made. The table showing the significant differences between graduate teachers and post-graduate teachers in respect of teacher stress in family.

TABLE -18

EDUCATIONAL QUALIFICATION	N	MEAN	SD	't' VALUE
1.00	92	29.27	7.68	0.781
2.00	108	28.43	7.44	@

From the above table the calculated 't' value is 0.781 found to be greater than the table value (1.96) at 0.05 level. Hence, the hypothesis-15 is accepted. Hence, there is no significance difference between graduate teacher and post-graduate teachers towards teacher stress in family.

5

Summary and Conclusion

It is high time to identify the problem of the teacher in particular his competency and his mental agony to make the teaching learning process useful to the present day condition. In the modern days teacher is loaded with so many sophisticated technological trends that were place in the modern human beings also confronted with many perplexing problems caused due to perpetually changing world resulting in frustration, Conflict, Anxiety, Stress and so on. Coleman in n1982 also observed that, "The 17th century has been called the age of enlightenment, the 18th century the age of reason, the 19th century the age of progress and the 20th century the age of anxiety". This emphasizes that a meaningful and satisfying way of life has become difficult in this age of anxiety the teacher of today is not exempted from the above age of anxiety.

Teaching is a sensitive weapon to achieve the expected educational goals through effective teaching learning process. The effective teaching is possible only with the teacher, those who are mentally sound. We should make the teacher away from the Anxiety, Stress and so on. So as to utilize all his teaching competencies to make the teaching learning processes in an effective way.

The modern research studies observed that the teacher performance and teacher behavior are strongly affected by stress. ARYACDU and SUTCLIFFE (1977) stated that," The stress with the teaching profession may affect the school as an organization, teacher performance, the physical and emotional well being of the teacher".

The modern research studies observed that the teacher performance and teacher behavior are strongly affected by stress. ARYACDU and SUTCLIFRE (1977) stated the, "The stress with the teaching profession may affect the school as an organization, teacher performance, the physical and emotional well being of the teacher".

MEANING OF STRESS

Stress is a condition stream on one's emotions, thought processes and physical conditions. When it is excessive, it can pretend once ability to cope with environment. (Hans Selye, 1976) "Stress is the general term applied to the pressures; employs developed various symptoms of stress as, "an adjective demand placed on the organism".

Stress has been defined following Lazarus's model, as a state of imbalance when the demands made on the person in different areas of life exceed her / his capabilities and resources (Lazarus and Folkman, 1984)

Stress has been defined following Lazarus (1974) as a state arising from imbalance between the demands made and the coping resources at one's disposal.

Stress has been defined as a state of imbalance between one's personal resources and the environmental demands, and manifested in the form of a number of psychosomatic factor, such as Somatization, Obsessive-Compulsive interpersonal sensitivity, Depression and Anxiety.

TEACHER STRESS

Job stress is most common psychological phenomena that is prevalent among people who are in different jobs and professions. The stress studies are initially directed toward industrial organizations within the private sector. Researchers have come to believe that stress may be especially prevalent among human service profession, particularly the teaching profession, (Kjyiacou and Suteliffe 1977-78; Pettegrew and Wolf 1982, Cherniss 1980: and Coorper and Marshall 1980). As a teaching is a human service profession, stress within the teaching profession is considerable and may have far-reaching consequences on the entire education system. Teaching is complex process were in teacher is expected to exhibit many skills. This makes a teacher to experiences stress in the profession.

Further, Pettergrew and Wolf (1982) opined that 'Teacher stress has a nationwide concern and relatively new area of empirical research".

Factors prepared by teachers as being troublesome or stressful have included students discipline, negative attitudes towards school, physical violence, is adequate preparation time, lack of clear role definition and heavy workloads". (Bearly, Myette and Serma, 1983; Chichen and Koff, 1978; Olander and Ferrel, 1970).

Teacher is subjected to stress due to incoherent social life, widening social distance, segregation, lack of societal support, corruption, nepotism, unnecessary societal involvement in day-to-day activities, high degree of social indiscipline, deterioration of values, lack of social security etc.

EFFECTS OF TEACHER STRESS

As job stress effect organizational performance, teacher stress impedes teacher performance in teaching. Infect it is assumed that mild stress can even enhance performance but high level of stress can create physical, Psychological and behavioral problems among teacher. There are several research studies, which observed that, a high level of stress accompanied by physical illness such as high blood pressures, ulcers and even cancer. Similarly high level of stress may be accompanied by psychological problems such as anger, anxiety, depression, nervousness, irritability, tension and boredom. Excessive stress may also result in behavioral problems such as sleeplessness, under eating or over eating, increased smoking and drinking and drug abuse. Many researches of teacher

TEACHER COMPETENCY AND STRESS-A BRIEFOUTLINE

The study is about teacher competency in relation to stress. Teacher competence, in general scene, impedes when teacher suffer from stress. In this chapter, a discussion is made about teacher competency, stress, and the development of this type of study in the world.

"Teacher competency" refers to the set of knowledge, abilities and beliefs a teacher possess and bring to the teaching situation. Teacher competence differs from teacher performance and teacher effectiveness in that it is a stable characteristic of the teacher that does not change appreciably when the teacher moves from one situation to another. It resembles teacher performance in that it has also been proposed as a basis from which teach effectiveness can be inferred.

NEED FOR THE STUDY

Accomplishment of educational goals and the objectives of teaching is possible only with the teacher those who are competent in teaching and free from any type of stress. Teacher stress directly or indirectly influences the competency of teacher in teaching. So the teacher who is subjected to stress may not be possible to teach properly which in term Indus is competency in teaching. Theoretically, this teacher stress may be heard to perform teaching in a competent way. But in practice how for teacher stress is influencing on teaching competency and to what extent teacher stress and teaching competency are related-are the questions waiting for answer. Hence, this study has taken up to find out how teacher stress teaching competency are inter related to each other in the context of high school education.

OBJECTIVES OF THE STUDY

1. To test the teacher stress and teaching competency scales to be use by the teacher himself.
2. To find out the relationship between teacher stress and teaching competency.
3. To find out the effect of demographical variables in respect of teacher stress.
4. To find out the effect of demographical variables in respect of teaching competency.

HYPOTHESES OF THE STUDY

1. There is no significant difference between Above 35 years age of teachers and Below 35 years age of teachers towards teacher stress.
2. There is no significant difference between Male and Female Teachers towards teacher stress.
3. There is no significant difference between Graduate teachers and Post Graduate Teachers towards teacher stress.
4. There is no significant difference between Above 15 tears, and Below 15 years teaching experience towards teacher stress.
5. There is no significant difference between Government School Teachers and Private school Teachers towards teacher stress.
6. There is no significant difference between Male and Female Teachers towards teacher stress in Professional growth.
7. There is no significant difference between Male and Female Teachers towards teacher stress in Work Load.
8. There is no significant difference between Male and Female Teachers towards teacher stress in Occupational Hazards.
9. There is no significant difference between Male and Female Teachers towards teacher stress in Student Behavior.
10. There is no significant difference between Male and Female Teachers towards teacher stress in Family.

11. There is no significant difference between Graduate teachers and Post Graduate Teachers towards teacher stress in Professional Growth
12. There is no significant difference between Graduate teachers and Post Graduate Teachers towards teacher stress in Work Load
13. There is no significant difference between Graduate teachers and Post Graduate Teachers towards teacher stress in Occupational Hazards.
14. There is no significant difference between Graduate teachers and Post Graduate Teachers towards teacher stress in Student Behavior
15. There is no significant difference between Graduate teachers and Post Graduate Teachers towards teacher stress in Family.

LIMITATIONS OF THE STUDY

1. The study is limited to only teachers of different schools in Chittoor of A.P.
2. Of the three criteria of teaching competency, only two criteria i.e. presage and process are covered in this study.
3. To measure the teaching competency and teacher stress teacher self –rating scales are used in this study.
4. Of many dimensions of teaching competency, planning presentation, closing evaluation, and managerial dimensions are considered in this study.
5. Of many dimensions of teacher stress professional growth, work load, Occupational hazards, Students behavior, family and societal dimensions are considered in this study

CONCLUSIONS

From the present study only one factor that is Educational Qualification as significant impact on teachers stress. The male teachers Mean value is 32.4348, which is more than Female teachers mean value (29.4907). The other factors are viz.,

1. There is no significance difference between Above 35 year's age of teachers and below 35 years age of teachers towards teacher stress.
2. There is no significance difference between Male and Female teachers towards teacher stress.
3. There is no significance difference between Graduate teachers and Post-Graduate teachers towards teacher stress.
4. There is no significance difference between Experience of above 15 years and below 15 years towards teacher stress.
5. There is no significance difference between Govt. school teachers and private school teachers towards teacher stress.
6. There is no significance difference between Male and Female teachers towards teacher stress in professional growth.
7. There is no significance difference between Male and Female teachers towards teacher stress in Work Load.
8. There is no significance difference between Male and Female teachers towards teacher stress in Occupational Hazards.
9. There is no significance difference between Male and Female teachers towards teacher stress in Student behavior.
10. There is no significance difference between Male and Female teachers towards teacher stress in Family.
11. There is no significance difference between Graduate teachers and Post-Graduate teachers towards teacher stress in Professional Growth.
12. There is significance difference between Graduate teachers and Post-Graduate teachers towards teacher stress in Work Load.
13. There is no significance difference between Graduate teachers and Post-Graduate teachers towards teacher stress in Occupational Hazards.
14. There is no significance difference between Graduate teachers and Post-Graduate teachers towards teacher stress in Student behavior.

15. There is no significance difference between Graduate teachers and Post-Graduate teachers towards teacher stress in Family.

Hence, there is no significant impact on teachers stress. Teachers would give more importance for the quality of education. It is necessary to encourage teachers to study for the further education. The role of Government is also important to motivate the teachers towards higher education.

SUGGESTIONS

EXERCISE: Physical exercise is accepted as the best antidote to stress. It keeps the body healthy, makes one emotionally strong, and eases nervous tension. It keeps the mind, body and action coordinated.

RELAXATION: Relaxation response is an innate physiological change elicited by some psychological means. Evidence indicates that the immune function in the body improves by relaxation training, and its regular practice can help maintain the cool. These can include hobbies like reading, listening to music, etc.

VALUE EDUCATION: Intervention for change in social and practical values can help them think and act rationally and proactively.

MEDITATION: It is a continuous scream of effortless concentration, on a single point, over an extended period. It is suggested that the concentration should be maintained unbroken. Psychologists have argued that meditation leads to better emotional and physical health.

YOGA: A stress management programme in the Indian setting may combine some elements of Gita and Yoga in the preventive plans. Srivastava (1981) concluded that persons coping more effectively with stress have more positive orientation to life in general, and employ a valuable mix of coping and defense response. Yoga is a holistic science, which gives to the person tools and techniques to expand conscious awareness into the unconscious In order to become aware of the patterns and tendencies that cause stress.

1. It is to be suggested that teachers effects teaching competency.
2. The stress creators harm the teacher effectiveness and teaching competency
3. The government or Private management of the institution should improve the conditions for better teaching by reducing the stress factors.
4. The main stress creators like lack of promotional opportunities lack of professional growth are to be tackled to improve the teaching competency.
5. Unless stress creators are reduced qualitative improvement teaching, learning process cannot be improved.

SUGGESTIONS FOR FURTHER STUDY

1. The study may be extended to higher and primary education.
2. To measure the teaching competency presage, process and product variables may be compared.
3. Stress and psychological well-being Among Tribal and Non-Tribal primary school teachers.
4. Stress and burnout among teachers in Regular and special schools.
5. Stress and coping among college students.
6. Stress and Coping among Adolescents.
7. Relationship between teaching competency and teacher motivation may be studied.
8. Relationship between teacher stress and teacher adjustment may be studied.
9. An extensive study is needed for teacher stress and teaching competency.

BIBLIOGRAPHY

1. Bailkeri, K. N. (1983): Effect of self- Instructional Remedial Micro Teaching course on the Instructional Competency of in service secondary school mathematics teachers.

2. Bhalwankar, A. G. (1984): A study of Reliability and Validity of the process appraising scale of teacher effectiveness.
3. Balachandran, E. S. (1981): Teaching effectiveness and student evaluation of Teaching, Ph.D., Education, Madras University.
4. Coates, T. I. and Thoresen (1976 spring): Teacher anxiety, A review with recommendation, Review of educational research 49(2), pp.159-184.
5. Cooper, C. Marshal, J. (1976): Occupational sources of stress. A review of the literature relating to coronary heart disease and mental ill health Journal of occupational Psychology, pp.11-28.
6. Cox, T. Mackay, C. J. Cox, S. Watts, C. and Brockley (1978): Stress and wellbeing in schoolteachers psycho-physiological response to occupational stress. Paper presented to the Economic Society Conference, Nottingham University England.
7. Dohrenwend, D. et. al (1981): Stress in the community a report to the president's commission on the accidents at three-mile land. Annual of the New York Academy of Sciences 365, 159-174.
8. Dac, R.C. Passi, B K. and Singh, A. (1982): Effectiveness of different strategies of integration of teaching skills in developing general teaching competency of student's teachers department of teacher education, NCERT.
9. Davis, H. (1964): Evaluation of current practices in evaluating teacher competency, in B. J. Biddle and J. Ellance (Eds). Contemporary research on teacher effectiveness, New York, Holt, Rinehart and Winston.
10. Donald, M. Medley (1982): Teacher Effectiveness" Encyclopedia of Educational Research, Education Harold. E. Mitzel, Vol. 4. Mac millan publishing &Co., New York.
11. Fimian, M. J. and Santoro, T.M. (1983): sources and manifestations of occupational stress and reported by full item special education teachers. Exceptional children, pp. 540-543.

12. Gupta, N. and Beehr, T.A. (1973): "Job stress and employee behavior", Organization behaviors and human performance, pp. 373-387.
13. Girdano, D.E. and Everly, G. S. (1979): Controlling stress and tension, Englewood cliffs, N.J. Prinetice hall.
14. Greenwood, G.E. Olejuik, S. F. and Parkoy, F. W. (1990): Relationship between four teacher efficiency belief patterns and selected teacher characteristics. Journal of research and development in education,23 (2), 102-106.
15. Gupta, S. (1981): A comparative study of Socio-Economic background problems and professional behavior of men women teachers in co-education Institutions at different levels in the state of Haryana, Ph.D., Education, Kurnool University.
16. Gupta, U. (1981): job involvement and need patterns of primary school teachers in relation to teaching effectiveness Ph.D. Education, All Universities.
17. Hodge, J. and Marker (1978): assuring teacher stress; Beneficial task for administrator, American secondary Education, 8(4).
18. Joseph schwrzwaldet at stress reaction of school age children to the Bombardment by send missiles journal of Abnormal Psychology 1993, Vol. 102, No.3, 404-410.
19. Kaiser, J.S. and Polezynski, J. J. (1982): Educational stress sources, reaction, preventions. Poe body journal of education 10.
20. Kessler, R. C. Price, R.H. and Wortman, C. B. (1985): social factors in phycho pathology, stress support and coping process, annual review of psychology 36, 531-572.
21. Kryiacane and Suteliffe, J. (1977): Teacher Stress; A review educational review 29.
22. Kryiacau, C. and Sutclifee, J. (1978): Teacher stress; Prevalence, Source and Symptoms, British journal of educational psychology 48.
23. Lazarus, S. Folkman (1984): Stress appraisal and coping, New York springer publishing company.

24. Lislie Sovoy (1990): "Source of stress on trainee lectures for further and higher education". Journal for Higher education summer (1990).
25. Vene, M.R. (1985): A study of some of the personality components of creative student teacher in relation to their competency towards teaching.
26. Yogendra Kumar and Rattan Lai (1980): Use of micro-teaching in improving general teaching competency of in service teachers.
27. Arnett, J.J. (1999): Adolescent storm and stress, Reconsidered. American Psychologist, pp. 317-326.
28. Folkman, S. and Lazarus, R. S.(1985): If it changes it must be a prosess: Study of emotion and coping during three stages of a college examination. Journal of personality and social psychology, 48, 150-170.
29. Lazarus, R. S. (1993): Coping theory and research: Past, present and future. Psychosomatic Medicine, pp.234-247.

Is conventional computer instruction ineffective for learning?

Recent research in the area of cognitive science indicates that traditional computer instruction, which requires learners to simultaneously attend to a manual, computer screen and keyboard, overloads working memory and interferes with the learning process. This paper reports on a series of studies which used a variety of computer applications in both educational and industrial settings and found that trainees following conventional computer instructional techniques could successfully work through a manual and complete the required computer based tasks yet learn very little (Chandler & Sweller, 1995; Sweller & Chandler, 1994). Alternative, cognitively guided manuals which physically integrated manual, screen and keyboard information and could be studied without the use of the computer were shown to be far superior learning tools than conventional computer manual instruction. This paper also reports on findings from ongoing research into other aspects of computer instruction including computer based training, multimedia presentations and the use of computer based animation. It will be asserted that conventional computer based training techniques may also incorporate many of the poor instructional design qualities that are a feature of conventional manual based instruction. Novel computer based training packages generated by cognitive load theory (Sweller & Chandler, 1991; 1994, Sweller, 1988; 1993), which appropriately focus attention and reduce mental load, may be superior training techniques. The same theoretical framework may also place multimedia instruction into a theoretical context and clarify how multimedia presentations should be structured. Finally, ongoing studies investigating the advantages and disadvantages of computer based animation will be reported and discussed.

How do we learn to use a new computer package?

Suppose you have just purchased a new software application and have successfully loaded it onto your computer. How will you now proceed to learn the new package? A number of options are usually available. The most traditional would be to consult the relevant manual and work through the instructions directly on the computer. This activity usually involves reading segments of text from the manual, memorising these details, while searching for the related information on the computer screen and keyboard before performing the required task. Another option would be to utilise a computer based training program that now accompany many new applications. In this case, the manual is not needed and learners only need to follow the required computer assisted instruction perhaps in the form of a tour guide, tutorial or a set of examples. Many of these packages convey instructional information in "text" boxes located at fixed positions on the computer screen. This textual information usually refers to information on the screen. The learner must then assimilate this information by matching the text with the related screen items.

Recent research in the area of cognitive science suggests that neither conventional computer manual based instruction or conventional computer based instruction, discussed above, are ideal training formats. Alternative instructional techniques based on our growing knowledge of human cognitive are now available and are demonstrating their superiority over conventional computer instruction. The same cognitive theory may also assist in the structuring of multimedia presentations and computer based animation.

Specifically, this paper has four objectives:

- To report on a group of studies which demonstrated that cognitive guided integrated training manuals were far better learning tools than conventional computer instruction (Chandler & Sweller, 1995; Sweller & Chandler, 1994);
- To discuss ongoing research comparing cognitive computer based training packages with conventional computer manual and conventional computer based instruction;
- To show how auditory/visual research (Mousavi, Low & Sweller, in press; Penney, 1989) can be applied to multimedia instruction and provide guidance into how computer based multimedia presentations should be structured.
- To reveal some of the cognitive implications of introducing animation into computer based training and to present some very recent findings demonstrating when it is useful and areas where it may be counterproductive.

Before dealing with each of these four sections, I will very briefly discuss the cognitive framework that directs this research.

Aspects of human cognition

We have known for some time that humans have a very limited processing capacity. For example, perhaps you are briefly shown a shopping list and ask to remember as many items on the list as you can. Chances are you will remember only a few items. Miller (1956) believed that our short term memory was limited to about seven chunks of information, while Simon (1974) claimed that the number of items people can process is closer to five. Cognitive scientists now favour the term working memory, a concept that emphasises an active centre where current mental activity takes place. While working memory is widely thought to be strictly limited, long term memory is generally regarded as a huge information store. Expertise in a range of areas from chess (De Groot, 1965) to algebra (Sweller & Cooper, 1985) can be explained by a superior level of domain specific knowledge in long term memory.

Information stored in long term memory is thought to be highly organised into cognitive constructs called schemas. In general terms, a schema can be viewed as a cognitive construct that categorises information in the manner with which it can be dealt. An enormous body of research in a diverse range of areas indicates that most organised knowledge is encapsulated in schemas. Besides being the fundamental building blocks of knowledge, schemas also have the function of reducing the burden on working memory. For example, we can rapidly read the text on this page as the words correspond to previously acquired schemas. We do not have to look at the detailed shape of each letter and use working memory to combine the huge variety of shapes into meaningful prose. We only need to look at some of the shapes and use our highly sophisticated schemas acquired over many years to fill in the rest. Thus, we essentially bypass working memory and making use of our long term memory. However, a child learning to read, without complex schemas, will have great difficulty processing this information through limited working memory.

A second learning mechanism that also dramatically reduces the mental load on working memory is automatic processing. Automatic processing (Shiffrin & Schneider, 1977; Schneider & Shiffrin, 1977) allows information to be processed automatically, with little or no conscious effort. Most learning tasks initially demand conscious effort with the transition from controlled to automatic processing requiring considerable time and practice. While schema acquisition is the essential component in solving similar problems and exercises to those learned, automation seems to be the key ingredient in transfer and dealing with novel problems

(Cooper & Sweller, 1987; Kotovsky, Hayes & Simon, 1985). Thus, schema acquisition and automation are major factors involved in skilled performance and learning.

Cognitive load theory

While many of the aspects of the human mental processing system discussed above are largely accepted, instructions are rarely constructed with these points in mind. Training programmes (including those in computer instruction) frequently overload the working memory of learners and in doing so hinder schema acquisition and automation, the two primary ingredients of learning. Cognitive load theory (Sweller & Chandler, 1991; 1993; Sweller, 1988; 1989; 1993; 1994) have utilised the above cognitive model as well as its own notions of information complexity to develop a range of alternative cognitively guided training techniques. Cognitively guided instruction has shown to result in far more rapid learning than traditional instruction in a range of educational and industrial areas including mathematics, numerical control programming, electrical engineering, biology, physics and CAD/CAM (see Chandler & Sweller, 1991; 1992; 1995; Sweller, Chandler, Tierney & Cooper, 1990; Sweller & Chandler, 1994).

Conventional computer manual instruction

The opening to this paper described the behaviour one usually engages when learning a new computer software application. It was noted that conventional computer manual instruction, involves the learner simultaneously attending to the manual and computer screen and keyboard, a phenomena labelled as the split-attention effect (see Chandler & Sweller, 1991; 1992; Sweller et al., 1990; Sweller & Chandler, 1991 for full discussion of the effect). Sweller and Chandler (1994) claimed that the split-attention effect, the continuous process of reading segments of text from a manual, searching for corresponding screen or keyboard entities and assimilating this related information would impose a heavy mental load on working memory and consequently hinder learning. The authors developed a self-contained cognitively guided manual which physically integrated manual information with diagrammatic representations of the computer screen and keyboard. The authors then compared an integrated instructional manual group which studied their material in isolation, a conventional manual group which worked through their material on the computer and a third group which also worked on the computer but with a self-contained integrated manual. The latter two groups worked on the computer until they successfully completed all the required tasks. Results from a number of studies using a variety of software packages indicated that a cognitively guided integrated manual group, which had no contact with the computer during instruction, demonstrated superior learning, as measured by written knowledge and practical computer skills, over the other two formats.

Applying cognitive load theory

Over the last few years there has been enormous emphasis placed on computer based training. For instance, most if not all, new software applications are now accompanied with some form of computer assisted instruction (e.g., tour guides, tutorials & examples), designed to teach learners how to use the application. Furthermore, computers are increasingly becoming the chosen instructional medium for many educators to present teaching and training materials. The studies reported in Sweller and Chandler (1994) showed that a cognitively guided computer manual which physically integrated related information was a highly efficient learning tool. Could these same cognitive principles be applied to computer based training? Conventional computer based training does away with a manual, but may still involve split-attention and unnecessary searching and matching of disparate information. For example, consider the user presented with a standard computer based training program to learn a new software application. Many packages convey instructional information in "text" boxes located at fixed positions on the computer screen. This textual information usually refers to various entities on the screen. For instance, a textual commentary for a spreadsheet training package may refer the learner to the diagrammatic layout of the spreadsheet. To understand this material, learners must hold relevant text in working memory while searching for the related diagrammatic entity on the screen. The goal of understanding the application can only be achieved by performing a series of mental integrations, an activity that is likely to impose a heavy extraneous cognitive load. Thus, we are faced with a typical split-attention situation, an instructional format known to be ineffective for learning. How can we reduce extraneous load yet maintain a computer based instructional format? One alternative would be to redesign the software application so textual commentaries are physically relocated in close proximity to related screen entities, resulting in an integrated computer based training format. Cognitive load theory predicts that an integrated computer based training package would provide the same advantages as integrated hardcopy computer manuals (Sweller & Chandler, 1994) and integrated instructions in non-computing areas (Chandler & Sweller, 1991; 1992; Sweller et al., 1990). The need to mentally integrate disparate sources of information may be eliminated, mental load reduced and learning enhanced.

The hypothesized advantages of cognitively structured computer based training packages are currently under investigation. Specifically, an integrated computer based training program for a commonly used windows package has been developed and is currently being compared with conventional methods of computer based instruction.

Structuring multimedia presentations

At present, there is much debate and discussion concerning multimedia technology. Yet a comprehensive explanation of when it is useful and how it should be structured and presented is not available. Our current research is involved in testing the conditions under which multimedia presentations are beneficial and putting findings in a theoretical context.

Considerable research into a cognitive phenomena coined the modality effect suggests that if instructions are communicated in dual information modes (e.g., auditory and visual) then working memory will be expanded and performance will be enhanced (see Penney for detailed review). This view is consistent with modern conceptions of working memory (e.g., Baddeley, 1992) and is supported by a considerable body of research. For example, Allport, Antonis and Reynolds (1972) found that people were better able to carry out two tasks if the two tasks involved different modalities rather than the same modality. Frick (1984) found that more items were recalled in a memory test if some of the items were presented in a visual modality and some in an auditory modality rather than all in a single modality. Findings such as these lend credence to the multiple modality, working memory hypothesis and indeed, suggest that the effective size of working memory could be increased by using multiple rather than a single modality.

More recently, Mousavi, Low and Sweller (in press) utilised geometry instructional materials and found that a dual mode instructional format which used both auditory and visual sources of information was superior to a visual only instructional format. The authors noted that while diagrammatic information should be presented in its natural visual mode, associated text could be presented just as easily in an auditory mode as a visual mode, with a distinct advantage found for an auditory presentation of text.

This finding has obvious, direct applications for multimedia presentations. multimedia computer based presentations, where learners hear explanatory text while viewing related diagrammatic screen information, may be preferable to equivalent visual only instruction. Both instructional formats involve split-attention, but a multimedia format uses dual modalities and consequently supplies an effectively larger working memory for learners to assimilate instructional material. Conventional computer based multimedia packages are also usually equipped with a facility where textual instructions are presented simultaneously in both auditory and visual modes. With this format, the learner can hear textual information, and see identical information on the computer screen while viewing associated diagrammatic screen entities. Cognitive load theory predicts that this format would be inferior to a standard multimedia format where auditory text is not repeated visually on the screen. Repetitive visual text is not necessary for understanding and processing this information when the information is already provided in an auditory mode, imposes an extraneous cognitive load on working memory. The visual text is functionally redundant and if attended to may interfere with learning. In fact, one experiment in Mousavi et al., demonstrated that an auditory text/visual diagram format was superior to auditory text/visual diagram plus visual text.

We are currently investigating the implications of multimedia instruction on a wide scale using detailed training materials in industry. Once developed, a series of studies will compare three types of computer instruction. A conventional visual diagrams and text format will be compared with two multimedia formats, namely, a visual diagrams/auditory text format and a visual diagrams/auditory and visual text format. It is predicted, that a visual diagrams/auditory text format will be superior to both a conventional visual diagrams and text format and a visual diagrams/auditory and visual text format.

Cognitive consequences of computer animation

As animation increasingly becomes a highly prominent feature of computer based training packages, there has been much debate in the literature over the role of animation in instruction (Mayer & Anderson, 1991; 1992; Mayer & Sims, 1994; Reiber, 1990; 1991). What is needed, however, is further research examining the important factors involved in animation and the conditions under which it is useful and the situations where it may be counterproductive.

Computer based animations may be useful for a variety of reasons. For example, animations can efficiently demonstrate how a system works, such as blood flow through the human body. Basic animation such as highlighting, flashing or simple movement may also be useful as it has the potential to reduce the search process for learners. For example, if a multimedia presentation consists of a very complex or unfamiliar visual component, then an auditory commentary may be more readily assimilated if the related visual entity is moving, highlighted or under some form of animation. For example, if an auditory narration for a spreadsheet training package states that the "the sum of cell A1 and A3 is inserted in cell C2" then the appropriate highlighting of the related visual entities may considerably reduce the search, reduce the working memory burden and aid learning. If no animation is available, the auditory commentary must be held in working memory until the learner searches and matches auditory items with related visual entities.

Cognitive load theory predicts that in instructional areas where there is a high level of screen search, incorporating basic animation into a multimedia presentations will be superior to equivalent multimedia presentations without animation. Will such animations always be beneficial? It is suggested that animation will only be useful if there is a high level of screen search. In instructional areas, where there is no search or trivial search, then basic animation such as highlighting or flashing may distract or misdirect attention and interfere with learning. Specifically, if there is no screen search or trivial search, it is predicted that a multimedia presentation without animation will be superior to the equivalent presentation with animation. In fact, we have very recent preliminary evidence to support these hypotheses. Using primary school mathematical materials in a multimedia computer task, it was found that very simple animation in high search areas (i.e., corresponding angles) was notably beneficial but in areas of low search (i.e., perimeter of a rectangle), animation had negative learning consequences. This is a very significant finding that requires confirmation and closer examination with a range of instructional materials. This is currently under investigation.

Conclusion

This paper has attempted to apply the most recent findings in cognitive science directly to computer instruction. It has been suggested that most traditional computer instruction may have been designed without taking into full account the cognitive capabilities of its users and consequently may restrict learning by overloading learner's working memory. A range of cognitively generated alternatives have been developed and have demonstrated their effectiveness over conventional computer instructions. In addition, the ongoing research discussed in this paper may lead to a range of alternative computer based instructional techniques based on sound cognitive theory.

Paper Presentation, CALICO '98 Symposium, San Diego, California, July 9, 1998 by Paul A. Sundberg)

References

1. Allport, D., Antonis, B., & Reynolds, P. (1972). On the division of attention: A disproof of the single channel hypothesis, *Quarterly Journal of Experimental Psychology, 24*, 225-235.
2. Baddeley, A. (1992). Working memory. *Science, 255*, 556-559.
3. Bartlett, F. (1932). *Remembering: A study in Experimental and Social Psychology.* New York & London: Cambridge University Press.
4. Chandler, P., & Sweller, J. (1991). Cognitive load theory and the format of instruction. *Cognition and Instruction, 8*, 293-332.
5. Chandler, P., & Sweller, J. (1992). The spit-attention effect as a factor in the design of instruction. *British Journal of Educational Psychology, 62*, 233-246.
6. Chandler, P., & Sweller, J. (1995). Cognitive load while learning a computer program. Manuscript submitted for publication.
7. Kotovsky, K., Hayes, J. R. & Simon, H. A. (1985). Why are some problems hard? Evidence from Tower of Hanoi. *Cognitive Psychology, 17*, 248-294.
8. Mayer, R. E., & Anderson, R. (1991). Animation needs narrations: An experimental test of a dual-coding hypothesis. *Journal of Educational Psychology, 83*, 484-490.
9. Mayer, R. E., & Anderson, R. (1992). The instructive animation: Helping students build connections between

words and pictures in multimedia learning. *Journal of Educational Psychology, 84*, 444-452.

10. Mayer, R.E., & Sims, V, K. (1994). For whom is a picture worth a thousand words? Extensions of a dual-coding theory of multimedia learning.*Journal of Educational Psychology, 86*, 389-401.
11. Miller, G.A. (1956). The magical number seven plus or minus two: Some limits on our capacity for processing information. *Psychological Review, 63*, 81-97.
12. Mousavi, S., Low, R., & Sweller, J. (In press). Reducing cognitive load by mixing auditory and visual presentation modes. *Journal of Educational Psychology.*
13. Penney, C.G. (1989). Modality effects and the structure of short-term verbal memory, *Memory and Cognition, 17*, 398-422.
14. Reiber, L.P. (1990). Using computer animated graphics in science instruction with children. *Journal of Educational Psychology, 82*, 135-140.
15. Reiber, L.P. (1991). Animation, incidental learning, and continuing motivation, *Journal of Educational Psychology, 83*, 318-328.
16. Schneider, W. & Shiffrin, R. (1977). Controlled and automatic human information processing: I. Detection, search and attention. *Psychological Review, 84*, 1-66.
17. Shiffrin, R. & Schneider, W. (1977). Controlled and automatic human information processing: II. Perceptual learning, automatic attending, and a general theory. *Psychological Review, 84*, 127-190.
18. Simon, H. (1974). How big is a chunk? *Science, 183*, 482-488.
19. Sweller, J. (1988). Cognitive load during problem solving: Effects on learning. *Cognitive Science, 12*, 257-285.
20. Sweller, J. (1989). Cognitive Technology: Some procedures for facilitating learning and problem solving in mathematics and science. *Journal of Educational Psychology, 81*, 457-466.

21. Sweller, J. (1993). Some cognitive processes and their consequences for the organisation and presentation of information. *Australian Journal of Psychology, 45*, 1-8.
22. Sweller, J. (1994). Cognitive load theory, learning difficulty and instructional design, *Learning and Instruction, 4*, 295-312.
23. Sweller, J., & Chandler, P. (1991). Evidence for cognitive load theory. *Cognition and Instruction, 8*, 351-362.
24. Sweller, J., & Chandler, P. (1994). Why is some material difficult to learn? *Cognition and Instruction, 12*, 185-233.
25. Sweller, J., & Cooper, G. A. (1985). The use of worked examples as a substitute for problem solving in learning algebra. *Cognition and Instruction, 2*, 59-89.
26. Sweller, J., Chandler, P., Tierney, P. & Cooper, M. (1990). Cognitive load as a factor in the structuring of technical material. *Journal of Experimental Psychology: General, 119*, 176-192.

ANIMATION RESOURCES

DEFINITION OF ANIMATION

Animation — including all moving images whether on television, cinema, or video clips incorporated into computer applications — involves subtle changes in a sequence of stationary images presented in time, the fourth dimension, giving the illusion of connected movement. The term is normally applied, however, to moving images designed either by hand or by computer.

The Computer Animation Dictionary (1989) defines animation as "[p]reducing the illusion of movement in a film/video by photographing, or otherwise recording, a series of single frames, each showing incremental changes in the position of the subject images which when shown in sequence, at high speed, give the illusion of movement. The individual frames can be produced by a variety of techniques from computer generated images, to hand-drawn cels." It is not real motion, but perceived motion.

Non-photographic, "camera less" animation is frequently cited in canonical lists of the wonders of the multimedia capabilities of modern microcomputers? e.g. "Multimedia allows text, sound, animation, video clips ..." — but it are rarely an object of research by instructional technologists or discussed at IT or CALL conferences. Visual aids such as still images and video are much more widely discussed in the literature, yet animation is equally a subset of the category of visual aids.

The goals of this paper are twofold: (a) to raise CALL practitioners' practical and theoretical awareness of where computer-generated animation might be appropriate in second-language instruction and (b) to alert CALL designers to the unconscious influence of static instructional metaphors on instructional design, to help them to add a fourth dimension (time) to the three (and often only two) dimensions in which they typically conceive of their task.

COMPUTER ANIMATION BASICS

Animation is older than motion pictures themselves. The first picture animation (hand drawn) was created on a spinning disk in 1831 by Frenchman Josèphe Antoine Plateau. It was not until 1906 that animation was added to celluloid film in the newly-born motion picture industry. The first computer-generated animations were developed on mainframe computers at Bell Labs in 1963; however, they continued the tradition of "camera less animation" begun earlier in the 20th century.

Animation deals not only with motion per se (its most obvious sense), but with any change in an object — change in position (i.e. motion), change in color (e.g. blushing), change in brightness, change in size, and metamorphosis — change from one object into another (e.g. caterpillar into butterfly).

Traditional animation of the Disney or Hanna Barbera variety is based on cels (images on transparent celluloid acetate sheets) that are then filmed at n cels per second to give the illusion of smooth movement. The cell concept was first developed in 1915 by American Earl Hurd. Computer animation is a term that covers a wider area than cell or key frame animation, however.

The computer can fill various roles in animation (Thalmann & Thalmann 1990:13):

(a) creating the basic images to be animated (digitizing or created with graphics editor) plus backgrounds
(b) adding motion to prefabricated images by generating trajectory paths for whole objects (in-betweening) or motion of components of objects (e.g. a person's hands) or otherwise transforming their shape, color or brightness
(c) coloring the images to create a realistic look
(d) synchronizing motion of the graphics with sound
(e) controlling a physical movie camera to record an animation sequence or following a virtual camera program
(f) editing and synchronizing animated film at the postproduction stage

In CALL, I assume most designers will be most interested in (a) through (d) since (e) and (f) involve professional-level motion picture production.

Computer-Assisted animation vs. Computer-Modeled animation

Computer-assisted animation, or key frame animation, is the type of animation most likely to be authored by CALL designers. It refers to creating two-dimensional graphic objects and animating them. Computer-Modeled animation, on the other hand, refers to creating three-dimensional objects and programming them with motion behaviors unique to each object.

Mode of generation: frame-by-frame or real-time

Computer animation can be generated frame-by-frame, then produced and saved as a "movie" (the Macromedia Director metaphor) or it can be generated real-time — on the fly according to user instructions as in rapid moving, interactive computer games or 3D virtual worlds (cf. "interactive dynamics").

Two-dimensional versus three-dimensional animation

Using the computer to create 2D animations is a faster method of creating the type of animations formerly hand-painted on cells. 3D animation, however, is an area where the computer shows clear superiority over hand-drawn animation since humans are very inefficient at drawing three-dimensional space, especially all the angles possible for viewing 3D objects.

"Man, in fact, has always found it difficult to represent three-dimensional space in drawings. It is simply impossible to produce all the tens of thousands of drawing needed for an animated film by hand. In this sense, the computer is not replacing man, since it does jobs which simply cannot be performed manually" (Thalman & Thalman: 61).

3D animation is computationally very complex, not only in the modeling of the static 3D object itself for viewing from any angle, but in programming the behaviors of each object in relation to other objects in the environment (e.g. two virtual people avoiding each other in passing).

Creating 3D human figures is especially tricky, since the human body can carry out such a myriad of actions. The human face with its many tiny muscles used in facial expressions is extremely complex to replicate by computer. Animation can create two forms of facial behavior: "emotions" (smiles, frowns) and "phonemes" — expressions directly related to producing speech (e.g. lip rounding, spreading, etc.).

Objects that can be animated

Beyond the stereotypical cartoon characters such as Bugs Bunny or Mickey Mouse, many other media can be animated: photographs (e.g. the opening animation sequences of Monty Python's Flying Circus), clay creatures, virtual 3D humans or human heads, individual letters in words, words/text in titles, film credits, etc., buttons, directional arrows and other cueing devices, transitions between "pages" or computer screens, and high-end, complex special effects to be incorporated into commercial films.

CALL designers are more likely to use the ready-made features in computer animation authoring systems to animate photographic images or simple geometric shapes than to design 2D or 3D cartoon characters from scratch — normally the task of professional graphic artists. Actions of human beings and animals would be more efficiently captured on video than painstakingly designed frame by frame in a computer graphics application.

STATIC VS. DYNAMIC INSTRUCTIONAL METAPHORS

Since many CALL practitioners/designers are themselves products of the pre-CAI era of education, they tend unconsciously to carry over a vision of instruction and certain expectations about instructional aids into CALL instructional design that reflect this experience. Younger SL students, however, have often been raised in a media environment with animated computer games, MTV music videos, movies and television — widely assumed to be "entertainment" media rather than educational media. By comparison, the static, traditional-appearing instructional presentations even in CALL-equipped language classes, for example, seem tame, less captivating to such learners.

Older instructional genres carried over? Consciously or unconsciously — into instructional design in computer-assisted instruction can be termed "instructional metaphors" — older genres for conceiving of new media. This is not necessarily negative. As Erickson (1990) points out: "metaphors function as natural models, allowing us to take our knowledge of familiar, concrete objects and experiences and use it to give structure to more abstract concepts" (p. 66). Operating systems designers, especially for Macintosh and Windows 95, have made profitable use of such older, more familiar metaphors in making the user interface more easily learnable: the "desktop" metaphor used in both OSs with trash/recycle, folders, files, etc. It is inevitable, perhaps impossible for instructional designers not to conceive of their product in older, familiar metaphorical ways. The question is: Is the metaphor appropriate? Is it optimal?

To begin a consideration of the merits of various metaphors for use in instructional design for CALL, the author offers the following examples of media metaphors (many familiar to language instructors) from pre-CAI days - static metaphors, dynamic metaphors, and a "hybrid" of the two? Along with sub metaphors ("pages" of a "book", for example) associated with each. None of the lists below are to be regarded as exhaustive.

- Static (unanimated) media metaphors, linear and non-linear:- The class lecture + blackboard/overhead transparencies/page of notes on handout (linear presentation) The textbook — computer as "electronic book" (A. Hubler) made up of "pages" (linear)
- The foreign language (FL) reader (collection of short stories, etc.)
- The FL grammar (systematic grammar reference)
- The newspaper + pages (nonlinear)
- The full-length scholarly paper + pages (linear)
- The stack of note cards (HyperCard) + cards (linear or hypertext)
- The map (nonlinear)
- The multiple-choice quiz + questions, pages (linear)
- The encyclopedia+volumes+pages (accessed nonlinearly, hypertext potential)
- The dictionary + pages (accessed nonlinearly)
- The photo album, coffee table book + pages (casually linear)
- The slide show + slides (linear)
- The magazine [casually linear]

Dynamic (animated) media metaphors

The following examples break out of the static metaphors above by incorporating live action sequences or hand-created animation:

- The live stage drama or play (one of the oldest metaphors dating back to Classical Greece and the rituals of preliterate societies)
- The music concert
- The cartoon animation (e.g. Bugs Bunny)

- o The full-length motion picture, seen either at a theater or on video
- o The filmed documentary
- o The television soap opera or telenovela
- o The television Sitcom (situation comedy)
- o The news broadcast or news reel (before television)
- o The live interview
- o The how-to program (e.g. cooking, home repair)
- o The television or movie advertisement

Hybrid metaphors

The term "hybrid metaphor" I uses to refer to media metaphors which, although traditionally static in terms of medium (usually paper-based), are based on dynamic, real-life experiences or stories. They are, in a sense, blue prints for dynamic media, much as Shakespeare intended his written plays to be performed. Computer-based multi-media (like motion pictures) can transform them into the dynamic versions from which they derive:

- o The script of a movie/play or opera libretto
- o The story/novel (in static form but with dynamic, linear content)
- o The foreign language "dialogue" (in static form on page but representing dynamic, real-life social interaction)

Animation is merely one presentation option currently allowed by multimedia-equipped computers and authoring applications. In instructional practice, it may be merely one element used within a static metaphor (an animated illustration of the workings of a flour mill in a digital encyclopedia, for example) or the entire metaphor of the program — a full-length animated feature (the equivalent of a digital Bugs Bunny cartoon) or acted play. In this period of synthesis, when formerly separate traditional and early 20th century media genres are being crossed and hybrid genres are resulting, an eclectic mix of static and dynamic media metaphors is to be expected and perhaps even to be welcomed!

There is a concomitant danger, however, that by mixing metaphors too radically, the initial advantage of the metaphor for the new learner is lost. Cates (1994) recommends that in such cases, a more encompassing metaphor be used that subsumes the two competing metaphors. For example, combining Beethoven's biography and animated musical selections might not fit comfortably into a book metaphor, but might fit into a broader metaphor such as the television documentary (subcategory: celebrity career retrospective).

MOTION AND HUMAN PERCEPTION/VISUAL COGNITION

Motion perception in the case of animation involves a psychological phenomenon known as "apparent motion", a human mental trait that creates an inner mental experience of smooth, continuous motion from a series of multiple static inputs that are perceived by the senses as "discrete and separate" (Sekuler & Blake1990: 269). A variant of the stroboscopic motion effect, apparent motion occurs when any object is seen undergoing incremental changes of position close enough together in space and time (roughly 24 cycles per second in film) to give the experience of motion, e.g. a row of theater lights that appear to be one light circling a marquee (cf. Small & Levinson 1989: 69). Visual perception research shows that the degree and smoothness of motion experienced in such apparent motion phenomena is dependent on factors such as image duration and timing, spatial proximity, similarity between objects in question, overall illumination level, and prior learning. Below a certain threshold level, motion is not perceived (S & L:72).

This optical illusion is equally created by motion pictures, video, television and cartoon animation. This paper assumes that what is said concerning the pedagogical role of computer-generated animation in CALL — and in instruction generally — applies equally to other media using similar optical trickery to convey motion, especially (in the case of CALL) digitized video clips. Secondary factors, such as different degrees of complexity of image in artificial and photographic animation, in the latter two cases, will undoubtedly be responsible for some differences in instructional effect.

Visual attention

Perceptual attention is highly selective: We can attend to only a small fraction of the complexity of our perceptual surroundings at one time. Our eyes move purposefully to take in key points to construct an inner map of the outside reality (Fleming 1987: 236). Moving objects have immediate perceptual saliency — they stand out from the static background, even when seen "out of the corner of the eye", in the region of peripheral vision. The visual center of the brain even contains direction-selective neurons sensitized to visual movement in a single direction. The perception of even a tiny amount of motion in a single direction allows attention to be drawn to it through neuronal cooperation that amplifies even weak signals (Sekuler & Blake:265-268). The ability instantly to pick out tiny motions, to judge the direction of the motion (trajectory), and to identify the source of the motion obviously have been an evolutionary advantage to many animals, including humans, both to locate prey and to avoid predators.

It is this evolutionarily useful predisposition to motion perception in humans that makes animation (a purely artificial motion source) one of the most salient of attention-getting devices — in instruction and elsewhere. "Changes, particularly in motion, are strong attention-getting factors. Sensitivity to these factors is present even in infants, hence the designer can use them with all ages .... Once attention is gained, continuing changes in the ongoing stream of instruction can help maintain it" (Fleming: 236). Endlessly repeating animations maintain attention, long after it is desired — compare the abuse of animated gifs on amateur Web pages that draw attention to themselves and away from the text.

ANIMATION IN EDUCATIONAL PSYCHOLOGY AND INSTRUCTIONAL TECHNOLOGY

One of the striking things when researching the use of animation in educational settings is the sparseness of the literature on it despite the relatively long use of computer animation in educational research (cf. Rigney and Lutz's 1975 study) and technology in general (since the mid 1960s). While much attention has been paid to comparing visual (graphic) vs. non-visual (text only) presentations (c.f. Paivio's dual coding theory 1987), little literature has dealt with the differences between static graphic presentations and animated graphic presentations. Rieber (1989) hypothesizes that "animated graphics should provide greater elaboration than static graphics when lesson information involves highly imageable, faces, concepts, or principles that change over time" (p. 6).

The findings on instructional animation have been mixed, however. Earlier studies tended to find animated instruction ineffective; only gradually are studies beginning to isolate various factors that may determine under which conditions animation is most effective (Rieber 1989). R feels, however, that such conditions are beginning to be defined: "...it is only recently that this research base has started to be effectively applied to instructional computer graphics...Research into animated visuals will require a similar systematic process and effort to uncover unique conditions." (R here compares the gradual elucidation of the optimal role of animation to the initial inconclusive and unencouraging research on static visuals, which later, more focused research showed indeed to have instructional value.)

Where instructional animation has been tried is primarily in the sciences, engineering, and math, where imaging of data and abstract principles is vital, e.g. to demonstrate Newton's laws of motion (physics), represent functioning of pumps (engineering), and visualize changes to variables in algebra word problems. Very little literature exists in which animation's role in Second Language instruction has been studied.

The theoretical case for visuals in instruction

Animated visuals are normally considered a subset of instructional visuals, and therefore research which applies to static visuals ought to apply equally to animated visuals (Rieber 1989).

One of the most frequently cited psychological theories to provide theoretical grounding for the use of visuals in instruction is dual coding theory (Paivio 1986 and elsewhere). Experiments in human learning and long-term memory have tended to support a dual coding model, but not a single coding model (i.e. a single mental representation is created from either visual or verbal modes), as claimed by Pylyshyn in cognitive science.

Paivio hypothesizes that there are two independent codes for creating memory: a verbal and a visual ("imaginal"), one activated by words and the other by pictures*. Retention of material can be increased if the information is initially coded in two codes rather than one. Thus, presentation in visual (including animation) and verbal modes simultaneously facilitates comprehension and memory formation (i.e. learning). If one memory channel is lost, as in the case of aphasia, the other remains. Moreover, the more concrete, or "imageable", verbal information is, the more likely it is to be dually coded in the brain. Concrete concepts can be stored both visually and verbally, whereas abstract concepts can be stored only verbally.

While research on the benefit of visuals in instruction prior to 1970 painted a mixed picture of their instructional effectiveness, since then research has more clearly defined what the facilitating conditions for their use (Rieber 1989:7):

(1) visuals are superior to words for long-term memory construction
(2) combining visuals with text facilitates learning, provided the visuals are related to the verbal content
(3) children under nine or ten rely more heavily on visuals than older students
(4) children's imagery abilities develop gradually, and children under nine or ten do not automatically form imagery when reading, necessitating visuals

Use of visuals plus text

One widely-studied area of research in educational psychology has been the relationship between text and visuals in instruction.

A purely graphical presentation may fail to aid comprehension since learners unfamiliar with the content may not be able accurately to perceive important, yet subtle differences (Rieber 1989: 9). "...animation without narration can have essentially the same effect on students' scientific understanding as no instruction (the control group)" (Mayer & Anderson 1991: 490).

The optimal combination of text and visuals appears to be the inclusion of a verbal description (in M&A's 1991 study, a verbal sound track) during the presentation of a (mechanical) animation rather than before the presentation (i.e. as an advanced organizer). Subjects who viewed the animation with a verbal description also did better than subjects who were exposed to the animation only or the words only. Similar results obtained for subjects viewing static visuals with text mapped to the illustrations: "effective understanding depends on words and pictures being coordinated with one another" (M&A: 484). Their study supports Paivio's dual-coding hypothesis, clearly showing the superiority of simultaneous use of both a visual and verbal code (building a referential connection between input from the two codes).

Intrinsic motivation and animation

Intrinsically motivating instruction is an ideal in designing instruction. Students who perceive themselves as in control of their success stay with a task longer and are more likely to return to it. External reinforcement (i.e. from the instructor) is less effective at motivating students. Motivation/arousal lies on a continuum, and optimal levels theoretically exist for various instructional components — including animation, Rieber believes (1989:13).

In Rieber's experiment contrasting text-only, static visuals-plus-text and animation-plus-text presentations, 4th graders were highly motivated to return to the animated presentation when given the choice of that over other computer and non-computer activities. Internal reinforcement (pleasure) proved a greater motivator than external reinforcement (praise for correct answers). For this age group, at least, animation proved an intrinsically motivating methodology.

Age factors in the effectiveness of animation

Age of subject was one influential factor Rieber noticed in his literature review of the use of animation in education. Studies using adult subjects (e.g. King's 1975 study of Naval training students 1975) tended to show that animation had an insignificant effect on learning, whereas studies with children tended to show its effectiveness. Adults, R hypothesizes are better at creating an internal visualization from text (imagery ability), whereas children are still developing this skill and thus rely more on visuals. After the age of nine or ten, imagery ability in children becomes more developed and they are thus less dependent on visuals for comprehension of prose.

Spatial aptitude factors and animation

Another significant learner variable in the effectiveness of animation appears to be the spatial aptitude of the subjects. In a study designed to find a correlation between success in learning from an animation and spatial ability, subjects with low spatial aptitude were found to benefit from animated presentation (again due to poor imagery ability), while subjects with high spatial aptitude showed no effect (Blake 1977). This suggests that spatial imagery ability varies widely even among adult learners and is an important learner variable in predicting the instructional effectiveness of animation.

Incidental and intentional learning using animation

Traditional instructional design in the systems approach aimed at intentional learning: specific instructional goals are determined, instruction is designed, and the student is given a narrow, goal-specific presentation. Incidental learning occurs when the student attends to secondary information, perhaps not consciously "taught", and learns material beyond what was planned by the instructional designer. Rieber's 1990 study showed that recall for incidental information improved with the use of animation. His subjects were not explicitly taught a particular law of physics, but were incidentally exposed to it through seeing animated depictions of objects exemplifying another of Newton's laws of motion. In spite of the lack of explicit attention to the other law, however, the secondary animation stayed with subjects and aided their physics reasoning in later tests.

Degree of interactivity of animation

Animation can be presented in two ways: (1) preprogrammed dynamics, in which the learner is a passive viewer of animation designed prior to showing (this includes all popular film animation such as Walt Disney cartoons) and (2) "interactive dynamics" (Brown's term 1983), in which the animation is created on the fly, manipulated by the viewer, as in computer simulations and many computer action games. Adults learn from either type about equally, whereas children benefit more from the interactive animations, perhaps because of the intrinsic motivation of the latter, Rieber speculates.

Animation's functions in instructional design

Animation is not merely a presentation strategy in instruction; it can play a wide variety of roles. The following functions of animation owe much to Rieber's taxonomy of animation in instructional design (1989).

(1) presentation strategy — "the most direct instructional application" (Rieber 1989)
(2) as a supplement to the text for illustrating concepts
(3) as a supplement to the text for examples
(4) interactive dynamic — a practice activity using interactive animations, discovery learning. The learner tests hypotheses, which the program visualizes for her/him (e.g. flight simulation) — provided learners perceive differences in the visualizations. Simultaneous coaching or verbal prompts may be necessary.
(5) conceptualization? the animation serves merely to remind the learner of
(6) previously learned concept; no new information is depicted
(7) feedback? the motivation generated by the novelty in animation can be useful in reinforcing correct responses;

however, the novelty of such feedback may unintentionally reinforce wrong answers, i.e. rewarding errors with interesting feedback; for all such feedback, the novelty eventually wears off

(8) attention-getting devices (e.g. blinking arrows)? should be used sparingly

(9) motivation/reinforcement

(10) cosmetics-making an attractive visual impression ("technocentric" design); however, the "novelty should be used to draw attention to the information to be learned, not to the novel elements per se" (Fleming: 236).

Optimal role of animation in instruction

Based on the findings mentioned above, a preliminary list of instructional guidelines for the use of animation in instructional design can be formulated:

(a) Animation is most effective when used for conceptually new material. Studies in which the use of animation supplemented material that was already very familiar to the student or in which motion was not an inherent part showed little significant difference over pure prose presentation (Rieber 1989: 9).

(b) Learners should have some familiarity both with animation as a medium and with the topic presented, at least at a rudimentary level to profit from the animation If the learners are total novices to the material presented, they may not be able to attend to the relevant presentation points in an animated presentation with no verbal cueing or other advanced organizers. Indeed, the more complex the animation is visually, the more likely such incomprehension by learners will be.

(c) The material which is illustrated by the animation should be at a learnable level for the intended audience. Difficulty level of the material is another significant factor in the ultimate success of animation. When used to present material beyond the level of subjects, animation showed no benefit, whereas animated instruction tailored to the ability level of students has shown significant benefit.

(d) Animation should be an inherent part of the material presented, not a gratuitous add-on. In material in which visualization, sequence, motion and/or trajectory were essential (e.g. Newton's laws of motion), the animated presentation strategy showed significant advantage over text-only (Rieber 1989:10). To generalize from this and other studies, in order for animation to benefit learners, motion should be an integral component of the material to be learned.

(e) Sequencing and presentation of instructional modes — text, sound and animation — need to be planned for maximum effectiveness. In presentation strategy, Rieber (1988) found that careful cueing of grade-school students to what to attend to in a subsequent animation, and chunking of the textual and graphic presentation into separate frames controlled by the student was superior to simultaneous presentation of text with graphics, which resulted in cognitive overload and inadequate attention being paid to relevant details. Careful control of the quantity of material presented at one time, on the other hand, made the material more comprehensible and learnable. Mayer & Anderson (1991), by contrast, found that simultaneous presentation of an animation with a verbal "sound track" was superior to sequential presentation: the sound track followed by animation. This seemingly contradictory finding may perhaps be explained by assuming (a) that the quantity of verbal and animated presentation was at a comprehensible level and (b) that printed text as used in the Rieber study may compete visually with animation, while sound narration may not compete with the animation. The gratuitous addition of animation to verbal material which it does not fit, however, shows poor instructional design and will likely show no advantage over other presentation modes. The opposite effect is likely: distraction and confusion.

(f) Children should benefit more from animation than adults, although there does seem to be some ancillary benefit to adults. (This may apply only to adults learning via animation in L1.) When Rieber conducted the same study on adult learners as he had on 4th graders, however, there was no significant difference for the effect of animation over static or verbal presentation. Response time on the post-test, however, was significantly faster for adults in the animated visual condition group, where it functioned as an aid in retrieval. These subjects also showed less need for additional practice and rehearsal than the static graphics and no graphics group (Rieber 1989:11).

(g) Allowing the viewer greater control over the animation results in more learning. Animation's "greatest potential", Rieber claims (p.12), may be in its use as an interactive dynamic, letting learners control the course of an animation by their input when they are "in the driver's seat," rather than passively attending to (or not attending to) a visual presentation.

(h) Computer-generated animation may be superior to video when greater simplicity of image and saliency of the focal point is critical to the instruction. "Realism per se is not necessarily a virtue in instruction...picture-mediator enthusiasts have sometimes overlooked the fact that abstraction is often the intent of instruction" (Fleming: 242). Video by its nature includes details (in background and foreground) that may not be focal to the material presented, whereas camera less animation allows the designer to abstract an image to its bare essentials.

(i) Animation should be created at a sufficiently professional level for its intended audience. As with any media developed in-house, animation which is crude and obviously garage-shop quality may not possess much surface validity in the eyes of a student. Ideally, computer animation should be of a sufficiently professional level so as not to distract from the material presented. Adults, as a more sophisticated audience for media presentation, would require a higher level of production quality than younger children.

LANGUAGE AND MOTION/CHANGE OF STATE

Natural language reflects the inner perceptual (and social) experience of human beings, including the perception of motion and change of state. Speaking simplistically, we experience the physical world as: (a) discrete objects (e.g. trees) with static attributes (The tree is tall.), (b) static relations between objects (The tree is beside the stream.) and? when the fourth dimension, time, is included? (c) objects with dynamic, changing qualities (The tree is turning green.), and (d) objects in motion (The tree is swaying.). These semantic propositions are realized in natural language by such universal linguistic categories as subject and predicate (NP VP) and noun and verb and in particular languages by particular linguistic categories, such as adjectives and prepositions (these latter categories are widespread among world languages but by no means universal).

The perceived distinction between static reality (3D) and changing/moving reality (4D) is indeed reflected in natural language, but not in a one-to-one correspondence with a particular grammatical category: e.g. "movement is expressed by verbs," as a naïve respondent might at first suggest. In reality, these linguistic functions are parceled out among a number of different parts of speech:

(a) prepositions of dynamic location: to, from, into, out of, onto, off of, etc. marked by distinctions in the case of the article and noun head in languages such as Greek, Latin, Russian, German: im (in dem) Geschäft (in the factory -dative case for static location) in das Geschäft (into the factory - accusative case for dynamic location)

(b) prepositions of time: during, after, before, since, until, etc.

(c) participial adjectives: graying (hair), developing (country), etc.

(d) verbs of motion: run, walk, nod, wave, etc. (but not all verbs) verbs of change of state: become, increase, weaken, etc.

verbs of repetition: drip, hack (cough frequently), etc. adjectival verbs: e.g. Arabic form IX verbs of color or disability: iHmarra - to become red, blush

(e) nouns of phenomena: rain, drip, lightning, etc.

(f) verbal nouns: destruction, collapse, arrival, departure, etc.

Beyond parts of speech, there are other facets of language such as verb tense and aspect (many languages are morphologically much richer in aspect than English) that deal with motion or change of state:

Tense: The tree fell. (past)

The tree is falling. (present) The tree will fall. (future) Aspect: The tree has fallen. (perfective? static condition due to past action) The tree is starting to fall. (inceptive? the action has just begun) etc.

Animation, although it is mentally processed via a visual, rather than a linguistic code (cf. Paivio's Dual-coding Theory), can effectively depict the one dimension of the physical world that traditional static visual aids leave untouched: time, the fourth dimension. "Animation, like any graphic, should be expected to aid the recall of verbal information when it serves to precisely illustrate a highly imageable fact, concept, or principle." (Rieber 1989:6)

Language and the Brain

In psycholinguistics, language is viewed as a multi-level, symbolic system linking audial (phonological) representations with semantic representations in the mind. Thus, every word in a natural language is dually coded as sound and meaning — and, for a literate native speaker of a language with a writing system, trebly coded: sound/ orthography/ meaning. In neurolinguistics, this dually or trebly linked mental structure has been established as having a biological correlate in the structure of the brain.

In addition to links between a sound and meaning representation for words, the meaning component of concrete words (stored in the brain in separate regions from abstract words (Allport &

Funnel 1981)) is further linked with perceptual memories of the real world as experienced through the five senses: sight (e.g. a seashell), hearing (a giggle), smell (barbequed meat), taste (honey), and touch (satin). Human language, by its nature, involves multiple links between different areas of the brain, linguistic and non-linguistic.

Motion information, associated primarily with visual input from the outside world (secondarily with motor input from a person's own physical motion) is stored in a region of the brain adjacent to the visual center and is presumably linked to lexical items dealing with motion. According to dual-coding theory (Paivio 1986), learning concrete vocabulary items simultaneously with their physical-world counterparts should improve both speed of comprehension and retention in Long Term Memory. In addition, with the appropriate stimulus following learning, the vocabulary associated with the stimulus should be retrieved from Long Term Memory more quickly. In the case of language dealing with motion and change of state, using animation as an initial presentation medium and as a memory stimulus should aid in the comprehension, storage and recall of such language in either the L1 or L2.

Where first- and second-language learning differs is that L1 learning involves a child building the initial schemata for language from scratch, linking audially-encoded words with their real-world referents and creating higher-level semantic linkages, according to the Schema Theory paradigm (Gagné & Glaser 1987: 62-63).

In the case of L2 learning, the initial linguistic schemata have already been created with their dually- and trebly-coded mental connections. L2 learning therefore involves linking new information with old, mapping a new linguistic code (the L2) onto a pre-existing, language-independent semantic framework. The novelty in using visuals in an L2 instructional presentation thus lies not in the visuals themselves (except perhaps when they depict culturally unique aspects of the L2 culture), but in the new linguistic code which is attached to them. The use of visuals, including animation, should thus aid in initial understanding and processing of the L2 linguistic code (learning) and subsequent retrieval of it, although initially, the L1 connections should be much stronger than the newly-formed L2 connections for the same stimulus (and L2 connection stronger than L3, and so on).

ANIMATION IN CALL

If the literature on the use of computer animation in instruction in general is sparse, the literature on the use of animation in Second Language instruction is even sparser. In a university library database search, I found only two related articles: an unpublished dissertation (Suzuki 1996) on "The Effect of Animated Hypermedia Instruction on the Appropriate use of postpositional particles by beginning college students of Japanese" (an empirical study) and a literature review (Xiao & Jones 1995) entitled "Computer Animation for EFL Learning Environments" (a literature review). Perhaps this paucity of written material is due to the fact that the technology for authoring with animation has become widely available to ordinary CALL practitioners only in the last few years. Much basic research, therefore, remains to be done.

Meanwhile, however, beyond the general guidelines for the optimal use of animation in instructional design (section 5.9), we may begin to ask what constructive role animation might specifically play in Second Language learning and instruction. Learning a second language involves mastering a variety of skills: intellectual (syntactic parsing and semantic construction via reading or listening), visual (interpreting a writing system), motor (controlling the muscles involved in the speech apparatus), and communicative. What contribution might animation make to such typical SL concerns as teaching L2 pronunciation, writing reading, syntax, listening and culture? Likewise, various competing SL teaching methodologies are currently in use; how might computer animation relate to these various methodologies?

Animation and second-language skill areas

In response to the first question, with what SL skills computer animation might be an appropriate teaching medium, I believe that the general instructional principle Rieber and others have frequently stated applies: To be instructionally sound, a dynamic/animated presentation format must be appropriate to the nature of the material presented, i.e. it must have a necessary time component with motion and/or change of state. In the section below, I review several traditional components of SL instruction in which such elements are found or where secondary advantages of animation may apply.

(a) **Teaching pronunciation** Traditionally, the teaching of L2 pronunciation has relied on static cut-away side views of the vocal apparatus to illustrate phonological production. However, pronunciation is by and large dynamic. In reality, producing the phonemes of any language involves a sequence of motions among various parts of the vocal apparatus: creating an air stream, manipulating various parts of the throat, tongue and lips to restrict or stop the flow of air. In the case of affricates such as [tsh] and [dzh], the tongue moves from one position to another to create the sound. Likewise, in the case of diphthongized vowels, movement is an essential component of the sound, e.g. movement towards lip rounding ([aw], [ow], [uw]) or constriction of the mid tongue and palate ([aj][ej][ij]). Static diagrams cannot do these inherently sequential actions justice. Traditionally, this lack in the textbooks has been made up for by the real-life modeling of the pronunciation by the instructor. A live human model is still optimal; however, some form of animation — either video clips of a real person pronouncing sounds or three dimensional animation using an animated human head — would approximate the dynamics of real speech more closely than the static illustrations in pronunciation texts. A further advantage of non-photographic animation is the potential to show simplified anatomical cross-sections of the vocal apparatus, highlighting only the relevant parts of the vocal apparatus.

(b) **Teaching the calligraphy / writing of differing L2 writing systems** For native speakers of Latin alphabet-based languages, much initial teaching time is taken up instructing them in the writing systems of non-Western languages such as Russian, Chinese, Japanese, Arabic, Hebrew and Hindi. For ideographic writing systems such as Chinese and Japanese, especially, writing each character requires scrupulously following a traditionally-ordained stroke order. Since writing is a dynamic procedure, illustrating ideographs with animation (as, for example, in Kanji Master software for Japanese) would be far closer to the end behavior than the static numbered diagrams of stroke order currently available to students.

(c) Teaching reading Of the language-related skills, reading is the most visual skill; in fact, reading is termed "visual language processes" in the psychological literature. Although the text itself is normally static, the act of reading itself (saccades of the eyes from word to word) is dynamic. It is natural, therefore, to look to a dynamic tool such as animation when a dynamic element is desired for L2 textual presentation. In computer-assisted L2 reading instruction, for example, animation allows a presentation style in which each printed word in the text is visually highlighted while it is being read aloud, coordinating the reader's eye movements with the reading speed of the audial track. However, the L2 reader should ideally be given some control over the speed of the presentation to keep the flow of verbal information at a comprehensible level. The above is not to imply that animation is appropriate for all instances of L2 reading, however. It is merely one potential means of reading presentation among many. More in line with Paivio's Dual-coding Theory, an animation could serve as a visual aid embedded in the text page to illustrate, say, a manufacturing procedure being discussed in the text. The animation should not, however, be running in an endless loop while the reader attempts (futilely) to concentrate on the text. Rather, a button should be provided to allow the reader to control when (and whether) to launch the animation.

(d) Teaching listening Although there is no visual aspect to listening per se, L2 learners depend on many contextual cues, including visual ones, to understand what they are listening to. Using dynamic visual aids to clue the listener in on the topic of conversation is a highly effective aid to L2 comprehension as an advanced organizer, taking advantage of existing schemata in the learner's mind to aid him/her in processing the new audial content. Another potential listening exercise with animation would be to present the listener with oral instructions which s/he would then follow by manipulating an animation? an interactive dynamic, in this case. The goal would be for the learner to demonstrate comprehension at each step by correctly matching the on-screen animation to the oral instructions—a CALL variation on the Total Physical Response methodology.

(e) **Teaching morphology and syntax** Animation could serve to highlight salient features in the L2 syntax: regularities in morphology (the conjugational endings of Romance verbs, for example) or various syntactic transformations (such as changes in word order in English question formation? He will come tomorrow. -> When will he come?). In addition to animation's innate attention-getting properties which can direct students' attention to such syntactic patterns, use of animation could help increase student motivation in a subject often considered one of the duller aspects of foreign language learning. Animation might also be used to illustrate tense and aspect distinctions in a second language by presenting a natural sequence of scenes without the highly abstract grammatical explanations often given in L2 texts. For example, to illustrate the English present perfect tense's relation to present time, an animation of a tree falling could be presented with a sequence of sentences: the tree is standing; the tree is falling; the tree has fallen; the tree is lying on the ground.. The grammatical features of the second language are can thus be acquired naturalistically in a meaningful context as in first-language acquisition.

(f) Teaching culture is one L2 content area where a pre-existing schema in the adult learner may be missing. Not only is the linguistic information new, the visual/experiential information has, as yet, no mental representation. Although an American student of Chinese, for example, may have a schema for festivals in general, it is doubtful that the term "Moon Festival" would stimulate any concrete associations in her/his Long Term Memory. The learner must construct a new linguistic and sensory schema from scratch — often with no opportunity in the US to experience that cultural element first hand. In this case, an animated "virtual" experience is the next best thing. For elements of culture which involve sequence, procedure, motion, etc. animation should be the preferred presentation mode when the "real thing" is unavailable. Cultural elements that qualify are festivals, games, gestures, dances, and religious ceremonies. However, as most of these involve human subjects — traditionally one of the hardest objects to depict graphically — the most efficient medium for capturing and displaying cultural content may well be videotape/film rather than computer-generated animation.

Animation and SLA methodologies

As for computer animation's role in different teaching methodologies, it is merely one computer-assisted instructional mode among several and not wedded to any particular methodology. As a basic (neutral) presentation methodology, animation is thus likely to find a role in a wide-range of SL and FL teaching methodologies: from grammar-centric approaches to natural language-, communication-centric approaches.

Grammar-translation approaches will see animation mostly as a means to illustrate aspects of syntax dealing with motion and change of state, and perhaps as a means of focusing learner attention on various linguistic forms, i.e. animated text.

More communicative methodologies, on the other hand, will see animation as a useful tool for presenting naturalistic settings where students provide the language: describing scenes, telling stories, interpreting the various communicative functions required in scenes of human interactions. Here the content of the animation will be much richer and more varied.

In a task-based instructional style, animation may be used to illustrate a totally non-linguistic topic. Students might watch an animation originally intended for native speakers of the L2 that illustrates how nuclear power plants operate, for instance, the goal being to learn new information through the second language. Again, the main criterion for choosing an animated presentation is whether the instructional objective includes motion as an inherent component.

New roles, new directions for the CALL designer

The CALL designer has primarily tended to think of her/his role as lesson-writer, textbook-writer, test-maker? traditional instructional roles. New authoring applications that allow longer-length animated presentation, as documentaries and cartoons have traditionally done, should encourage CALL instructional designers to experiment with new roles, such as that of animator or movie director. In this new role, the CALL designer is free to break out of static instructional metaphors and begin to conceive of larger play-like productions involving characters, plot, and dialog . Plays are proverbially a metaphor for real life ("all the world's a stage"). If real language reflects the totality of human life, perceptions, and emotions, then L2 materials ought more closely to mirror that totality. Animation (and digital video) adds the time dimension.

With the advent of 3D virtual worlds on the Web and elsewhere, CALL designers should soon be able to develop more open-ended, less instructor-guided L2 learning environments? interactive dynamic worlds? where learners can select, even design, their own characters and settings and spontaneously create their own plots and dialogues. Learners will be able to play make-believe doctors and patients in virtual hospitals, function as CEOs of foreign corporations in virtual office buildings, and travel through virtual galaxies in virtual space ships as astronauts. The possibilities are no longer limited by the technology, but by the preconceptions of the instructional designer.

QUESTIONS FOR FURTHER STUDY

Given the relatively infantile state of research on animation in CALL, a number of questions arise from the existing literature on animation in general and findings on second language acquisition.

1. How should the verbal half of the word/image dual-input best be presented in SL instructional contexts with animation: as printed text, as an audible sound track, or as simultaneous sound and printed text?
2. Animation has proved effective in presenting cognitively new content in fields such as physics and engineering. Does this same advantage apply to animation in second language learning, which involves mapping a new linguistic code (L2) onto previously learned concepts and human experiences — leaving aside for the moment the issue of very real cultural differences in experience of life.
3. Both computer-generated animation and digitized video allow a four-dimensional presentation mode. Are they processed cognitively in similar ways? How are they alike and how do they differ? Human-designed animation gives the instructional designer the advantage of being able to control the amount of visual complexity in the moving images and backgrounds, whereas video often includes much irrelevant, and potentially distracting naturalistic detail. On the other hand, video photography is often less expensive and labor intensive than camera less animation.
4. Do Rieber's observations about age-difference factors in the effectiveness of animation on L1 learners also apply in a second-language instructional setting? What age of L2 student would most benefit from animated presentations? Are adult L2 learners cognitively similar to younger L1 children in the effect dually-coded presentations have on them?

REFERENCES

1. Allport, D. A. & Funnell, E.. (1981). Components of the Mental lexicon. In *The Psychological Mechanisms of Language.* London: The Royal Society and the British Academy (published jointly).
2. Blake, T. (1977). Motion in instructional media: Some subject-display mode interactions. *Perceptual and Motor Skills,* 44, 975-985.
3. Brown, J. (1983). Learning-by-doing revisited for electronic learning environments. In M. A. White (Ed.), *The future of electronic learning* (pp. 13-32). Hillsdale, NJ: Elrbaum.
4. Erickson, T. (1990). Working with interface metaphors. In B. Laurel (Ed.), The art of human computer interface design (pp. 65-73). Reading, MA: Addison-Wesley.
5. Fleming, M. L. (1987). Displays and Communication. In R. M. Gagné (Ed.), Instructional Technology: Foundations, (pp. 233-260). Hillsdale, NJ: Erlbaum.
6. Gagné, R. M. & Glaser, R. (1987). Foundations in learning research. In R. M. Gagné (Ed.), Instructional Technology: Foundations, (pp. 49-83). Hillsdale, NJ: Erlbaum.
7. King, W. A. (1975). A comparison of three combinations of text and graphics for concept learning. (Report No. NPRDC-TR-76-16). San Diego, CA: Navy Personnel Research and Development Center. (ERIC Document Reproduction Service No. ED 112 936).
8. Mayer, R. E. & Anderson, R. B. (1991). Animations need narrations: An experimental test of a dual-code hypothesis. Journal of Educational Psychology, 83, 484-490.
9. Mayer, R. E. & Anderson, R. B. (1992). The instructive animation: helping students build connections between words and pictures in multimedia learning. Journal of Educational Psychology, 84, 444-452.
10. Milheim, W. D. (1993). How to use animation in computer assisted learning. British Journal of Educational Technology, 24, 171-178.

11. Paivio, A. (1986). Mental representations: A dual-coding approach. New York: Oxford University Press.

12. Rieber, L. P. (1988). The effects of computer animated lesson presentations and cognitive practice on young children's application learning in physical science. Unpublished manuscript.

13. Rieber, L. P. (1989). A Review of Animation research in Computer-based Instruction. In Proceedings of Selected Research Papers presented at the Annual Meeting of the Association for Educational Communications and Technology. Dallas, Texas. (ERIC Document Service No. ED 308 832).

14. Rieber, L. P. (1990). Effects of animated visuals on incidental learning and motivation. In Proceedings of Selected Paper Presentations at the Convention of the Association for Educational Communications and Technology. Dallas, Texas. (ERIC Document Service No. ED 323 943).

15. Rigney, J. & Lutz, K. (1975). The effects of interactive graphic analogies on recall of concepts in chemistry (Technical Report No. 75). Washington, DC: Office of Naval Research. (ERIC Document Service No. ED 109 639).

16. Roncarelli, R. (1989). The Computer Animation Dictionary. New York: Springer-Verlag.

17. Sekuler, R. & Blake, R. (1990). Perception. New York: McGraw-Hill.

18. Small, E. S. & Levinson, E. (1989). Toward a theory of animation. The Velvet Light Trap, 24, 67-74.

19. Suzuki, T. (1996). The effect of animated hypermedia instruction on the appropriate use of postpositional particles by beginning college students of Japanese. Unpublished dissertation. University of Texas at Austin.

20. Thalmann, N .M. & Thalmann, D. (1990). Computer animation: Theory and Practice. Tokyo: Springer-Verlag.

21. Xiao, X. & Jones, M. G. (1995). Computer animation for EFL learning environments. In Eyes on the Future:

Converging images, ideas and instruction. Selected Readings from the Annual Conference of the International Visual Literacy Association. Chicago, IL. (ERIC Document Service No. ED 391 518).

Index